To those brave military women who have given their lives so that future generations may continue to enjoy freedom and liberty. Their sacrifice is an inspiration to every American, military or civilian, man or woman.

The Woman's Guide to Military Service

Texe Marrs and Karen Read

Second Edition

LIBERTY PUBLISHING COMPANY
Cockeysville, Maryland

Published by:
Liberty Publishing Company, Inc.
50 Scott Adam Road
Cockeysville, Maryland 21030

Library of Congress #83-82659
ISBN 0-89709-152-3

Cover photos:

Courtesy U.S. Air Force,
U.S. Navy

Manufactured USA

Table of Contents

Preface

WHY THIS BOOK WAS WRITTEN

"I wish I had read this book *before* I joined the service." This is what women now in the military have told us after reading this book, which is the first comprehensive guide to military service written especially for women. The previous lack of such a guide has meant that women who entered the military did so in a knowledge void. Only a recruiter—usually male—is available to answer the many questions posed by prospective women recruits. That's why we wrote *Everywoman's Guide to Military Service*—to help women truly and fully understand what military life is like, *before* they commit themselves by contract to three, four, or six years of military service.

We believe the armed forces have much to offer a woman concerned about her future. Each branch of service offers training and education opportunities, good pay and benefits, the adventure of travel, and the excitement of meeting new friends. The military also offers a commodity unobtainable in most civilian careers—the intangible but real reward one gets from knowing she has contributed to her nation and to society. This contribution is the vital one of defense of our country, its freedoms, and our way of life.

Nevertheless, military service is not for every woman. Membership in the armed forces presents a challenge to prospective members, and being a part of the military team means hard work, dedication, and personal sacrifice. Not everyone can measure up. Consequently, over one-third of all women who enlist end up being separated from the military before their term of service is completed. Some just can't maintain the high standards of the service. Others find military life far different from what they thought it would be. Uninformed about women's roles in the armed forces, these women become disillusioned and fail to advance in their jobs or training. They are "casualties" of military service.

This book will help you avoid being a similar casualty. We have a combined 28 years of military service. As veterans, we know what the service is really like. To gauge the feelings and attitudes of women and men now in uniform, we have visited Army, Navy, Marine, and Air Force installations. Much of the information in this book comes not from official sources, but instead is based on the reality experienced by the hundreds of servicewomen and men who frankly discussed with us what their branch of service means to their lives.

How can this book help *you?* If you are seriously considering either enlisting or accepting a commission in one of the armed services, here are just a few questions you need answered *before* you sign-up:

- Is the military a suitable career for women?
- Do the armed forces offer women equal opportunity with men?
- What does the military have to offer a woman? Why should I join?
- What jobs/occupations are open to women?
- What about boot camp for women?
- What are the disadvantages—the negatives—of military service for women?
- How can a woman best succeed and get ahead in the armed forces?
- How does the military handle special concerns of women . . . like pregnancy, personal health, family, and other matters?
- What do women now in uniform have to say about their lifestyles?
- What do *servicemen* think about the women who work side-by-side with them?

We answer these questions—and more—in *Everywoman's Guide to Military Service.* We want you to know exactly what awaits you once you have accepted the military challenge. Thus armed with sufficient knowledge, you will be able to make an intelligent and informed decision on whether the military fits your own life and career goals and aspirations.

Women in the Military

Is the military a suitable career for women? Women themselves obviously believe the answer is *yes.*

"We are continually swamped with inquiries and visits from women interested in the Navy," says Chief Petty Officer (CPO) Warren Smith, a U.S. Navy recruiter in Austin, Texas. "The military is highly popular with today's career-minded women."

CPO Smith's comments undoubtedly could be echoed and endorsed by all of the more than 5,000 recruiters of the five armed services: Air Force, Army, Coast Guard, Marine Corps, and Navy. The military is increasingly viewed by women as an excellent means to attain career goals, acquire valuable training, and achieve upward mobility in life.

Just how popular *is* military service among today's ambitious, able women? Last year alone, military recruiters received almost a million queries from women seeking information about the armed forces. Not surprisingly, there were three women applicants for every military job opening.

Glamour magazine in a recent poll asked its readers their views toward military service. A large majority—*61 percent*—said they "would consider military service." An even greater *72 percent* believed the military to be "a good career for women," and an overwhelming *78 percent* thought "there should be *more* servicewomen."

These statistics reflect the keen interest women have in military service. They provide convincing proof that contemporary women no longer believe the military to be the exclusive province of males. Regardless of the fact that women are still excluded from combat-related jobs, women have discovered the many opportunities offered to those who agree to serve their country in uniform.

What's more, the outstanding performance of women who have served and are now serving in our armed forces has caused a widescale reversal in public attitudes. A few decades ago, a vast majority of the public felt strongly that a woman's place was in the home and not, by any means, in one of the armed services. Not so today. While people still debate whether women should be sent into combat, there is little opposition to women serving in support roles. Indeed, only a few hard-core traditionalists would deny women the right and the opportunity to serve. Even those few opponents would find it hard to refute the great body of evidence that military women have made and are making tremendous contributions to the effectiveness of our armed forces.

Those who do believe women out-of-place in the armed forces generally feel that the military is "no place for a lady." To them, the military is a males-only preserve, a macho-land with a rough and tumble lifestyle unsuited to womanhood. When they see a woman marine, sailor, airman, or soldier, their cliché response is likely to be, "What's a nice girl like you doing in a place like this?"

What women *are* doing in places like the Army, Navy, Marines, Air Force and Coast Guard is serving their country—and doing so admirably. Make no mistake—the armed forces *need* women. Some males and other women may not agree. They are wrong.

Our armed forces need competent people, men *or* women—people who can be trained and who have the capability to carry out a variety of important tasks. These tasks range from typing administrative reports to paying vigilant attention to radar screens that would detect an enemy missile attack. Without trained women in uniform to fulfill many of these important tasks, our armed forces would be about 200,000 people short. That's how many women the United States now has in its armed forces.

The fact is that neither femininity nor masculinity have much to do with competence. There are capable and competent servicemen and also similarly able servicewomen. Either category is prized. When a professional military leader has a job to get done, she or he wants to know that the person assigned to accomplish the job is competent, *period*! The issue of femininity or masculinity is of no consideration.

We emphasize this point because one of the greatest myths prevalent today is that women, being so-called "feminist creatures," simply don't have what it takes to get the military job done. This myth is often internalized by women in our society and it becomes a debilitating handicap, an artificial barrier to military achievement and success. Women who believe in this myth, even subconsciously, often limit themselves and their potential.

The authors have met quite a few women military leaders—colonels, admirals, and generals. As a group, they do not at all fit the stereotype of the rough, all-business, disciplined Prussian female. A few would remind you of kindly grandmothers—which they are. Others have charisma and that sense of business acumen we associate with professionals and leadership.

Like men, women come in all shapes and sizes and are configured in a number of emotional and psychological packages. Some women are brusque, direct, and could be considered by many to be "unfeminine" while other women take a softer personal approach identified by some as "feminine." Either type of woman might be competent.

In deciding whether military service is for you, you can safely discard the myth that military life is masculine and that there is no place for women who are feminine. There are plenty of factors you should consider in making a choice of military service. This isn't one of them.

Women's Superior Performance

If you, like many women, are bothered by a nagging fear that, perhaps, the military is not a suitable place for women, the performance of the 200,000 women already wearing green, blue, khaki or white service uniforms should quickly dispel such worries. Consider, for example, the fact that those military people who perform the best win earlier promotion in rank. Then take heart in statistics which show that in every branch of the armed forces, enlisted women are being promoted earlier than men. This is true for almost all enlisted grades.

Women are doing so well in the armed forces that a good many are re-enlisting once their initial term of service has expired. The most recent Department of Defense figures reveal that 56 percent of all women decided to re-enlist, compared to only 52 percent of the males. Apparently, military women are more proud of their achievements and more satisfied in their jobs than are the men with whom they serve.

It's Your Decision

The fact that women now in uniform are performing well and enjoying their work might encourage you to join their ranks. If so, great. But, of course, before you make that decision there are a lot of factors you should consider. The bulk of this book is devoted to helping you make that decision about military service. In the following chapter we will discuss the positive advantages of the military lifestyle; and subsequently, in Chapter 3, you will learn of the many jobs and occupational areas open to women. In later chapters, we will examine some of the disadvantages—the negatives—of military service and talk about the special concerns of women and how they are handled by the military. We encourage you to read this material carefully to gain a broad understanding of what military service entails and the challenges and opportunities that await women who enter our armed forces.

Before you make that final decision of entering—or not entering—active military service you will want to read here the profiles of several successful military women, like Major General Norma Brown, commander of one of the Air Force's largest training centers, or Ensign Brenda Robinson, the first black female to become a Navy pilot. These inspirational women are role models, servicewomen whose performance deserves to be emulated and whose advice definitely should be heeded.

At the end of most chapters are comments by service women and men on active duty. These excerpted comments are taken from actual letters to the editors of *Soldier, Sailor, Airman, Marine (SAM)* magazine, a monthly Department of Defense publication. The comments reflect a cross-section of views and perceptions held by armed forces personnel about the issues and topics discussed in the preceding chapter. However, the comments do not necessarily reflect our views.

Why do we present quotes of both women and men? Simply because the opinions and attitudes of both groups need to be expressed and understood to gain accurate insight into the nature of military service.

Also, you will find in this book a brief look at the evolution of women in uniform. You will discover that for over 80 years, women have ably and professionally blazed the historical trails of military duty. The list of women who have served well in peacetime and in war is long. Many women in the past have given the ultimate—their lives—in proud service as members of the U.S. Armed Forces. It is to these women that we dedicate this book, knowing that many of you reading it will take their place and continue to demonstrate that competence, patriotism, and dedication are qualities of both women and men.

A company of women in the Navy Recruits stand in formation at the Naval Training Center in Orlando, Florida (Naval Photographic Center).

Comments from Military Women and Men

"I believe women in the military serve well and have, thus far, distinguished themselves through the years. I respect women in our military and treat them with the respect they deserve, based upon their own individuality; I personally don't believe women should serve on ships, in combat, nor be subject to the draft. There is no need to draft American women into combat now, and there's never been a need to do that in the past. Our men of America are still sound of mind and body, brave and true."

—Petty Officer 2nd Class Fred Blackly
USS Fort Snelling

"I'm proud to be an American! If it comes time to lay my life on the line, I must fulfill my commitment. This country has been built around certain freedoms and equalities. That's why so many people have died for it. Doesn't that make you a bit proud to know that our women are willing to die for it too?"

—E-3, Navy
Destroyer Sailor

"At the time I enlisted in 1978 I came in for one reason, a job. As the end of my first tour neared I realized, that maybe I wasn't really in for the money (the pay's better now than it was in 1978). It became something I had to do, because I just like the word freedom, and knowing the government doesn't control me like a puppet. You are a soldier 24 hours a day, 7 days a week, 365 days a year. The military is what *you* make it."

—Army Sp5 Mary A. Gutreuter

"Women are here to stay. During every crisis in our country's history, they have done their part, they have stepped forward, unasked, to serve their country."

—E-7, Marine Corps

"To all of the Bozos who feel the military is no place for women: You ought to either get used to the idea or get out. They are here to stay, guys. I, for one, am proud to serve with them. As for combat duty, if you had your act together, you would find that Title 10 of the U.S. Code says that women are not allowed in combat. They're not excluded from the armed forces. So stop complaining to the women about it and place the blame where it belongs, on Congress. Personally, I would rather go into combat with more of the women I know than men. Hang in there ladies, there's still a lot of us males rooting for you."

—E-6, Navy

"In the Marine Corps, we have our men and some boys. And I'd rather have a woman than a boy. Ten years in the service—you learn a lot."

—Staff Sergeant
Marine Corps

"On May 27 I will be a civilian again. Not just any civilian, though. I will be a civilian proud to have served in the United States Air Force. Proud to have served under good and not-so-good circumstances. The day I separate, there will be no fancy change of command ceremony, brass band, or 21-gun salute; however, I'll walk out the main gate knowing I did my best! Every time the band plays 'The Star Spangled Banner,' or when the flag's unfurled, I'll be standing tall."

—E-4, Air Force

"As a civilian working for Uncle Sam, I have seen all sides of the service. If service personnel would put aside the prejudice that a woman should stay at home barefoot and pregnant, this country would not have to worry about a threat from overseas. We would be held together as we were during the Revolutionary War when we fought for freedom. As I once read in a magazine, 'American ends in I can.' "

—GS-4 Susan M. Turner
Ex-SSgt, USAFR

"The military is a knowledgeable adventure if you want it to be . . . just like any other occupation, you get out of it what you put into it."

—Seaman (BT1) John Winfrey
USS John F. Kennedy

"There are no men or women in the service—only sailors. I personally think women sailors have more leadership and set a better example for others. Just because most women sit behind a desk and take care of all the paperwork, they are still a very important part of the military. If it weren't for paperwork, where would the services be now? I feel women should have the same opportunity as men to go to sea. I would feel a lot better working beside someone I can depend on. The majority of the women in the service are dependable and reliable."

—E-4, Navy
San Diego, CA

"I gather from talking to students that they want an option when they get out of college besides just the civilian job market or they want to better prepare for a civilian career . . . If they do go back to civilian life, they're doing so as more responsible citizens."

—Col. Howard Stiles
New England Coordinator, AROTC

"Civilians supposedly make double the money I make. The problem is getting a job in civilian life. I read about electricians like me making $30,000 a year. I went home on leave and tried to get a job. All I was offered was about $12,000 a year. I make more than that in the Army."

—SFC Roger Brillend
Ft. Hood, TX

Why Join The Service?

Annually, over 350,000 men and women enter the military service. Today the 2.1 million members of our nation's armed forces are all volunteers. Although there is talk of reinstituting the draft, since 1972 no-one has been pressed into military service against their will. All of these two million plus volunteers chose the military profession because they valued the opportunities it offers.

Why Join the Service?

The Pentagon has conducted a number of studies to determine why women volunteer for military service. The striking result of one study was that women seem to be more motivated to "get ahead in life." According to a Department of Defense survey reported in the Spring 1982 issue of *Reflections* magazine, many more women than men chose as their reason for joining the "opportunity to better myself."

When asked for specific reasons, women most often cited the opportunity to acquire job experience and training.

MOST IMPORTANT REASONS FOR ENLISTING

Reason	**Male**	**Female**
Job experience and training	50%	51%
Employment (pay and benefits)	21%	18%
Adventure and travel	11%	17%
Patriotic commitment	12%	11%
Military career	4%	2%
Respect for military tradition	2%	1%

Figure 2-1

Each of these valid reasons for choosing the military way of life deserves comment.

Job Experience and Training

Maybe you've seen on television the popular military recruiting ad which boldly trumpets: "We don't ask for experience, we give it!" For a young person with no marketable skills and without a college degree, this promise of acquiring valuable job experience and training may prove irresistible. Even college graduates may be lured by the attraction of receiving training in vocational skills or job experience in a marketable field. This is particularly true if the individual's college degree is in a field, such as history or English, not directly related to the world of work. However, even those who hold degrees in engineering, business, computers, and the hard sciences may find the job experience offered by the military to be of great value to civilian employers.

It is a well-known fact among civilian job recruiters that individuals with service experience are more likely to be hired and to receive higher pay than those without military work experience. Also, authorities in business and industry generally rate military-trained employees as more mature and more capable than their non-military peers.

The military services offer training and work opportunities in a vast number of job and career specialties, from heavy equipment operator to personnel and administration. Many of these specialties are directly transferable to the civilian job market. Thomas W. Carr, in *The Changing World of the American Military,* stated that 85 to 90 percent of military skills can be related to civilian occupations. This is especially true of the so-called blue collar fields—those specialties of a technical or skilled vocational nature. These include jobs available in electronics, computer repair, automotive repair, telephone equipment maintenance, plumbing, carpentry, and heating/refrigeration. The military also has jobs in white collar fields that pay substantial salaries in civilian life—jobs like computer programming, personnel, air traffic control, weather forecasting, photography, and intelligence.

The Civilian "Catch 22"

Many of these military job fields are virtually "off-limits" in the civilian market to persons with no experience. A person may tire of hearing civilian employers' constant refrain of, "Come see me when you get some work experience." It's the traditional "Catch 22": to get a job initially, you must have *had* a job and *have* job experience.

Unlike civilian firms, the military offers the chance to acquire both training and actual work experience in many valuable civilian skills. Equally important, the individual receives compensation while in training and important educational benefits under the Veterans Administration once her service commitment is over.

The Largest Campus in the World

It is a tremendous undertaking to train the 350,000 new people who annually enter the service. Also, 2.1 million personnel already in uniform must be kept current in their jobs by continued training and frequent refresher courses. To accomplish this training, the armed forces operate what is, without question, the largest campus in the world. It is a campus that consists of huge training complexes staffed with the most modern equipment and highly qualified faculty.

Military training classes are offered at nearly every military site—even in remote areas of the world such as the Aleutian Islands and lonely Johnston Island in the Pacific.

Many military installations are devoted entirely to training purposes. For example, the Air Force operates seventeen air training command bases, located throughout the United States. The largest, Lackland Military Training Center in San Antonio, Texas, has a uniformed population of over 35,000 and trains people in basic military subjects, security and police, science and cryptology (transmission of secure communication), foreign languages, and a host of other programs. The Army, Navy and Marine Corps operate equally impressive training centers, some which rival large state universities in size.

The Quality of Military Training.

Military training is equal to or superior to what's available in civilian communities. The quality is such that the same accrediting agencies that judge the acceptability of civilian university courses and technical/vocational curricula have also accredited many service schools. What this means is that often you may be given actual college credit for successfully completing a military technical school or training course.

The Air Force even has a congressionally approved Community College of the Air Force—it's own two-year, fully accredited college. If you finish an Air Force course, you automatically receive a transcript awarding you college credits. You can then transfer these credits to virtually any civilian institution.

Whereas the Air Force has its Community College, the Army proudly has a unique and widely applauded apprenticeship program. As a soldier learns her job and demonstrates proficiency, her supervisor documents it on an official log form. When the new apprentice is rated fully qualified—often both a written and a performance test is required—the Army applies to the U.S. Department of Labor for a Certificate of Completion of Apprenticeship. This certificate can be a powerful tool the individual can use in seeking a civilian job. It also is a mark of achievement which helps the person advance in her Army career.

Earning a College Degree

In addition to job training courses and instruction, all the services encourage their personnel to enroll in college courses while off duty. To accommodate the many people seeking a college degree, every military installation has an Education Center that offers free correspondence courses and resident college courses. Also, servicewomen may receive college credit by passing challenge tests called DANTES (Defense Activity for Non-Traditional Education Services).

DANTES exams are offered in a wide range of courses—

English, mathematics, history, education, astronomy, etc. which correspond to actual college courses. If you pass the DANTES exam, many civilian colleges will award credits just as if you successfully completed the course on campus.

You may also be glad to hear that college courses are offered on almost every military installation, stateside and overseas. The Navy even has what it calls the Floating University—college instruction is provided sailors on ship, while at sea.

Reputable civilian colleges conduct the courses and provide both the professors/instructors and the textbooks. Schools like the University of Utah, Park College, the University of Nebraska at Omaha, the University of Maryland, North Carolina State University, and many other recognized institutions participate in military education programs.

Now, the best part of all: your military service will pick up practically the entire bill for you if you choose to go to col-

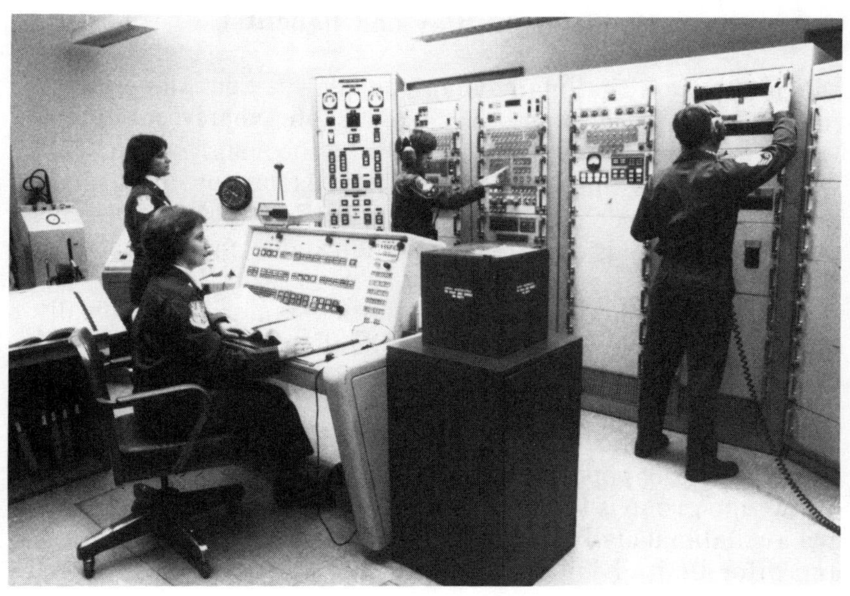

Four 308th Strategic Missile Wing Crew Members at work (U.S. Air Force).

lege part-time, after work. They'll pay at least 75 percent of your tuition and fees and sometimes as much as 90 percent! How many civilian employers can top that?

A "Way Station"

It is understandable that women would find in the service an opportunity to better themselves by acquiring valuable and marketable job skills. For many, the military is viewed as a "way station"—a place where they can get ahead and surmount impossible or difficult barriers encountered in today's civilian job market. After an initial tour of duty—normally three or four years, these individuals reenter the civilian economy trained, skilled, and ready to compete. However, for a great many other people, there is more involved to enlistment than a long-term goal of training and experience. There is the real and immediate need to find work and get that regular paycheck.

Employment (Pay and Benefits)

It is apparent that many young people seek out the military recruiter simply because they need a job. Nearly one out of every five new women recruits state they sign up for this reason. Perhaps this is not a romantic reason nor does it hold the glamour of such incentives as travel and patriotism. But the economic needs of many young men and women often leave them no other alternative.

Unemployment among young adults in America is typically higher by a wide margin than that found in any other segment of society. During the height of the 1981-83 recession, the U.S. Labor Department reported a huge 40 percent unemployment rate among Americans aged 18-21—quadruple that of the overall working population. Even in good times, the joblessness of this age group is typically in the double-digit area. Jobs that are available usually pay little more than the minimum wage and offer limited job security and benefits.

Thus, the economic security of the military looms large in many an unemployed young person's mind. The promise of a guaranteed job, relatively generous benefits, and a policy of "no lay-offs" holds great appeal for a person without a permanent job or who had a job but was laid off.

However, it's not only youth alone who look on the military as a haven in times of economic distress when unemployment is soaring or as a job opportunity for those without marketable skills. Recruiters around the country, especially in economically hard-hit areas, find that older adults as well are today gravitating to the military in search of a secure job. The maximum age for enlistment ranges by service—from 26 in the Coast Guard to 35 in the Navy (see Figure 2-2)—and recruiters report that the median age of applicants is higher than ever before.

MAXIMUM AGE FOR ENLISTMENT

	Enlisted		**Officer**	
	Men	**Women**	**Men**	**Women**
Coast Guard	26	26	26	26
Army	35	29	35	29
Navy	35	35	35	35
Aviation			29	29
Nuclear Power			27 1/2	27 1/2
Diving-Strategic Weapons			29	29
Air Force	29	29	35	35
Medical Doctor			35	35
Nurses			32	32
Marines	27	27	28	28
With prior service	32	32	30	30

Figure 2-2
(Source: Military Recruiting Services)

For example, it is a common occurence for a divorced woman in her late 20s or early 30s with dependent children to apply for military enlistment. Also, the recruiters are now seeing more *couples* in this age group, in situations where both are unemployed, or perhaps under-employed. As with the younger set, these people believe the military a good bet to find self-improvement and job training, while earning a decent if not great salary.

Salary

In case you're wondering just how much that "decent if not great salary" is, here's what you can expect to receive each month in military pay immediately after enlisting:

Base Pay	$668.40
Housing Allowance	123.00
Food Allowance	135.00
Total	$926.40

If you're going in as an officer (usually graduates of college ROTC, one of the service academies, or of an officer candidate school), your total pay will be considerably more—about $1,435 per month.

Now, in the case of enlisted persons, these figures are for married personnel. If you're single, you'll probably find that you'll be given free on-base housing (if a shared, marginally decent room can be called housing!) and a meal card which you can use to eat for free at the military dining hall. In return, the money you would otherwise get for housing and food allowance will be withheld and kept by the government.

However, married service people are permitted to live off the installation in the nearby civilian community, and the service will pay them the full housing and food allowance.

Is the military thus unfair to enlisted singles? You bet, but it's cheaper this way since the military has a huge investment made in on-base singles dormitories and enlisted dining halls.

Pay Increases

It's important to note that your pay will increase the longer you stay in the service. Pay is based on both seniority and on your military rank, or grade. You'll probably enter the military in the E-1 pay grade (O-1 if officer), unless you've had prior military training or agree to enlist for as much as six years.

The exact title corresponding to the E-grades varies by service. For example, in the Army, an E-1 is a private; in the Air Force, the equivalent title is airman basic.

Within a year, most women get promoted to E-2. A year later—a year-and-a-half in the Air Force and Marines—you'll be an E-3. At each higher pay grade, your pay will increase.

Starting at $926 a month, pay typically increases to $1,080 after two years of service, to $1,275 at the four year mark and continues to the sizeable sum of $2,635 for 26 year veterans. In 1983, officers' pay ranged from the $1,435 for an O-1 to $4,480 or more for a long-time (26 years plus) career officer. Military pay is usually increased annually to keep up with inflation.

Special Pays

Military pay is also supplemented by a variety of valuable special pays. First, there's a tax benefit: the money you get for food and housing allowances is non-taxable, meaning more cash in your paycheck. Then there are these special pays to which you may be entitled: flight pay, hazardous duty pay, diver's pay, sea pay, and proficiency pay.

Also, enlisted personnel receive a small clothing allowance—about $6 to $12 per month. Finally, there are overseas cost of living allowances, and foreign service pay—which women at some overseas bases may receive.

All these special pays and allowances can add up to a handsome sum: some personnel receive several hundred dollars per month in these supplemental amounts.

Enlistment and Reenlistment Bonuses

In addition to the regular and special pays and benefits, some military people find themselves in the enviable position of being handed thousands of dollars just to sign-up for military service. Then, a few years later, they may again be offered a cash inducement to reenlist.

Enlistment bonuses are paid only to women who enlist for more than the minimum number of years and then only if they enlist in a specific career field—usually a hard to fill specialty. A specialty that's hard to fill is often one that's either undesirable, or else *so desirable* that servicepeople in that skill leave the military to accept higher paying civilian positions in the field. This creates vacancies and, to attract qualified applicants, a bonus is offered.

As of 1983, the Army was willing to give bonuses of up to $5,000 for those entering fields such as intelligence and electronics. The Navy was shelling out $2,000 upfront to people who signed up for communications and jobs of boiler maintenance, sonar technician and radar repairer.

Reenlistment bonuses are paid to people who agree to reenlist in a hard-to-fill, critical career field. Up to $20,000 may be yours if you are in such a field at reenlistment time. That's the maximum, though, and most re-up bonuses are considerably less—in the $4,000 to $7,000 range.

Fringe Benefits

Equally as important are the generous fringe benefits offered by the services. One of the most important is medical and dental care. You're 100 percent covered. If you are married, the medical expenses (though generally, not dental costs) for your spouse and children are also covered. If military medical services aren't available, you'll be allowed to use civilian doctors and medical facilities, and Uncle Sam will foot the entire bill. Also, your military pay continues while you are ill or under a doctor's care.

Another benefit that married people especially appreciate is the military's subsidized commissaries which offer groceries and toiletries at cut-rate prices. Everything is priced at wholesale, and a small 5 percent surcharge is added at the cash register. Studies show that commissary patrons save as much as 29 percent on their groceries.

Two other benefits are life insurance and retirement pensions. Life insurance policies are available in the amount of $35,000 for only a few dollars a month. As for retirement benefits, even if you are young and you're not contemplating retirement for many years, you will be pleased to know that the military retirement system is at no cost to you. Whereas almost every civilian plan requires a hefty contribution from its participants, the military, in effect, pays this for its people.

How generous is the military retirement plan? Very! If you spend at least 20 years in uniform and you achieve the highest enlisted grade (E-9) while on active duty, you could leave service and receive over $900 per month for the rest of your life. If you stay in the military for 30 years, that figure would jump to nearly $1,400. Officers receive more—the average officer would get about $1,530 after 20 years and $2,300 after 30 years service.

And get this: if you're, say, 18 when you enter the service, you can retire at the youthful age of 38. Twenty-five now? You can start drawing that retirement check at the early age of 45.

Join the Service . . . See the World!

As valuable as job security, career training, and pay and benefits are, these factors are not the only motivators for military service. The lure of travel and adventure attracts thousands to the military.

This reason for entering the service is found among entrants from the cities, rural areas, and the suburbs. In the core of the cities, youth often find conditions so fretful that military life looks extremely attractive by comparison. Likewise, rural youth often join the service to escape what they consider a dull, routine life on the farm or in a small town. Middle class women tired of bland suburbs also find the travel and adventure option too good to pass up.

All the services extol the values of travel and adventure offered the military person. Navy recruiting campaigns are famed for their appeal to persons who, for instance, find excitement in the Navy's exhortation to "See the World—Join the Navy." The posters and ads do not, however, allude to the monotonous and quite dull, everyday life experienced aboard ships and submarines. Still, it is true that the Navy, as well as the other services (except the Coast Guard), offers unique opportunities for travel and adventure.

Some Navy ships, for example, visit as many as 20 overseas countries in the short space of one year, giving sailors and Marines travel opportunities second to no other profession. The Army and the Air Force also offer the thrill and joy of overseas adventure, with bases and posts located throughout the globe. In exotic locations like Hawaii and Bermuda, as well as faraway sites like the Azores and Okinawa, one can find thriving communities of U.S. military personnel.

Do you like to ski? Then perhaps the Olympian heights of Bavaria would suit you just fine. There are both Army and Air Force installations nearby. Do you yearn for the surf and the sun? Then, how about the sun-drenched beaches of Spain or Italy? Again, the military may be more than glad to accommodate your tastes.

A Patriotic Commitment

There is no doubt that millions of Americans consider military service a patriotic duty: a unique and special way for a person to serve her or his country. In this view, the individual sacrifices her time and energies in order to repay the nation, at least partially, for the privileges and benefits of freedom and liberty she is accorded.

The huge rush of volunteers—including thousands of women—to military induction offices in 1941 and 1942 after the Japanese attack on Pearl Harbor is indicative of the patriotic spirit displayed by a concerned American citizenry. The famed World War II and 1950's recruiting poster of a sober Uncle Sam pointing his finger and declaring, "Uncle Sam Needs You," is an example of a campaign designed to take advantage of national patriotic sentiment.

This desire to serve one's country is still a strong motivator of many people today. As a result, a good number of women seek to enter the armed forces out of a devotion to patriotic ideals. The sentiment of these youth is to put into action the words of Daniel Webster who in 1834 proclaimed, "God grants liberty only to those who love it and are always ready to guard and defend it."

Many programs are designed by federal and state governments to demonstrate the nation's gratitude for the sacrifices made by military men and women. For example, the Veterans Administration offers a variety of educational, medical, and loan guarantee benefits for veterans, as do many state governments. The federal statute requiring military draftees be reinstated to their previous job status by civilian employers is also indicative of attempts to recognize the military person's contributions, as are monetary bonuses paid to veterans by many states.

The Military Career

Probably few enter military service with the idea of making it a full, life-long career. Only 2 percent of the women polled gave this as their reason for enlisting. Yet, there are thousands of active duty military personnel who are careerists. In addition to the satisfaction of serving their country, the government often rewards generous benefits to those who reenlist and stay in for the long haul.

One advantage of a long-term military career is the increased promotion opportunity. Seniority gained by added years of service brings increased promotions, greater responsibility and authority, and more pay. Another advantage is the very generous retirement pension we discussed earlier.

The high esteem in which the public holds career military people is yet another factor in deciding on a career past the required initial duty period. America has always accorded great honors to its military heroes and leaders. Sergeant York in World War I and Sergeant Audie Murphy in the second World War were widely admired and respected. Each was awarded the Medal of Honor and lauded in the press and even in movies which told their story.

Also well-known and acclaimed are the professional careerists like General Douglas MacArthur, General Dwight Eisenhower, and General George Patton. These were men who spent almost their entire adult life in uniform: MacArthur served for 51 years, and Eisenhower, 52; Patton died while still on active duty at age 60.

Today, lack of opportunity may preclude women from winning the Medal of Honor or advancing to the high status of an Eisenhower or MacArthur. But conditions are rapidly changing and someday in the future, deserving women will, in fact, win such honors and recognition.

Military Traditions and Discipline

Finally, there are those who have a fondness for the tradition and disciplined life-style of the armed forces—the pomp and ceremony, if you will. Admittedly, the "spit and polish" military atmosphere, the strict adherence to authority required by some services, and the marching, inspections, physical demands, and other facets of traditional military life are not everyone's cup of tea. A tiny one percent of the women gave this reason as an important one for their joining.

Still, some enlistees do find the camaraderie, teamwork, and discipline the military represents desirable and satisfying. The demands made on the military person in this respect are similar to those required of champion athletes, musicians, university band members, and law enforcement personnel.

The emphasis on insuring its people stay physically fit and mentally alert is part of this military tradition of discipline. The sedentary lifestyle is out for uniformed personnel.

So, if you're a jogger or a physical fitness fanatic, you'll love the military service. If not, well . . . as long as you're in at least passable physical condition, you can tolerate the military's embrace of exercise and running regimes.

Oh, by the way, if you decide to enlist and you're *not* in good physical condition right now, don't fret. Boot camp is designed especially for you. The folks there are old pros in shaping-up fresh recruits. And they'll work on more than your body.

The entire military organization is designed to structure people's lives and render them receptive to old-fashioned military tradition and discipline. Obviously, this is an arduous task because Americans just don't seem to appreciate the negative features of military life. That's why we have a lot of fun spoofing the stuffy and authoritarian military lifestyle with television and movie characters like Private Benjamin, Marine Gomer Pyle, and the folks of M*A*S*H.

Still, the military is very insistent on molding its new recruits in the desired image. Chapter 6 is devoted to examining just what you can expect in this regard if you decide to accept the military challenge.

Army MP assigned to the 56th MP Co., Ft. Richardson, Alaska (U.S. Army).

Comments from Military Women and Men

"I joined because I wanted to travel and experience life as it really is. I didn't want to get into a 9 to 5 job, to sit there until I died of old age. I can't say I have enjoyed the whole experience, but life isn't always a party, good times, and a lot of fun."

—Seaman (AK2) R. G. Wheeler
Patrol Squadron 16
FPO New York 09501

"I asked for the Atlantic coast and they gave me California. Maybe the personnel clerk didn't take geography in high school!"

—A1C John Homan
Mather AFB, CA

"At first I dreaded summer camp. I didn't like the thought of getting up at 5 a.m. and running a mile every day. But it was fun."

Jennifer Swann
AFROTC Cadet Commander
University of Alabama

"I am proud to be a U.S. citizen and a member of the Armed Forces. You may use my name proudly."

—A1C Connie Gaylor
Kelly AFB, TX

"I gave up a job paying $1500 a week to join the Air Force. I was a lighting designer and technician on movie sets for movies. I was on the set of *The Electric Horseman* and *Superman II.* Unfortunately, although I was making quite a bit of money, I was only employed about 6 months out of the year. That's why I joined the Air Force—security. Show business is very fickle."

—AB Jeffrey M. Horvath
Lackland AFB, TX

"As a black woman, I hope to go to law school then go in the Air Force. There are so many blacks in the military and few blacks to represent them."

—Tamara Miller
AFROTC Cadet, Notre Dame

"Why did I join the Navy? If you don't love this country enough to support her, no matter what, go give the Soviet Union a try."

—E-3 Tristan Hopkins
NAF Midway Island

"You better believe I came in the Air Force cause I wanted to get away from home. Who wouldn't want to leave Vinton, Louisiana?"

—Airman Rodney Frehling
Dyess AFB, TX

"The recreational facilities and programs here are outstanding . . . they bring in a lot of shows and entertainment—Paul Williams, Red Foxx, and the Lettermen, for instance—and provide many different ways for people to have fun. My job is in an office so I now take aerobic dancing classes on base."

—Denise White
Sr. Airman, Clark AB, Phillipines

"I hated the Air Force, so I got out after four years. Boy, was I in for a surprise. Civilian life isn't a plum. I came back in the Air Force when I realized all the bums were on the east side of Chicago—civilians!"

—Sgt. Thomas Potter
Kessler AFB, MS

"At sea it's just us, the ship, and the elements. The camaraderie among the crew is foremost. It's a fantastic and very special experience."

—PO/2 Class Mary R. Laroche
USS L. Y. Spear

"I joined the Army and signed up for 6 years. The $1500 cash bonus and the student loan forgiveness program of the Army greatly influenced my decision to enlist. I will enter the journalism field in the Army."

—Veronica Puncohor
Ft. Jackson

"I came in the Air Force with no college. After going to college on base for four years, I got my Associate degree. Now, I'm in the AECP program and I will get an officer commission. I say the opportunities are unlimited if you want to improve yourself."

—Sgt. Dan Sellers
Brooks AFB, TX

"I don't do any more or less for the Navy than I would for a civilian employer. When I work, I work. When I play, I play . . . I enlisted because I wanted to, just like my father, brother-in-law, and brothers."

—Seaman (ADR1) Thomas Robinson
USS John F. Kennedy

"I think the Air Force offers educational benefits, challenges, travel, and exciting work."

—Cadet Ssgt. Cynthia Sexton
AFROTC, Purdue University

"Of the 27 sailors here on shore duty . . . the consensus is that everyone enlisted for basically the same reasons—job training for the outside, travel, and adventure. The overwhelming majority *re-enlisted* because they like their job."

—Petty Officer
San Diego, CA

"Being overseas you get to work with a different Army, learn lifestyles of another country, make friends."

—PFC Pat Lucite
Hq CO., 18th Infantry

Jobs for Women

Imagine coming across the following help wanted ad in the classified section of your local newspaper:

> **WANTED:** 33,500 women this year for vacancies in 636 job areas, including computers, electronics, administration, nursing, jet engine repair, and public relations. We train. Generous pay and benefits.

Sound too good to be true? As a matter of fact, the five branches of military service are at this moment making this exceptional job offer to American women. Even though barred from combat-related career fields, women will find that there is a virtual cornucopia of military jobs areas open to them: 636 in all.

Women's Sterling Performance

While a few die-hard chauvinists may feel women are being given military jobs which should go to men, the majority of men in uniform are appreciative of their female team members. From interviewing and talking with hundreds of servicemen, we find a positive attitude about working with women and a strongly perceived admiration toward military women. Generally, men are now convinced that women can be depended on as steady performers, capable of withstanding the stress and strain of military life and coming out winners! And this genuine upgrading in the status of women is not found only among young male service members.

Many an old-time sergeant was skeptical when women were "shoved down their throat" in the 70s and assigned jobs held formerly only by men. But the dependable and often even brilliant job performance turned in by many women has caused many a veteran to enthusiastically support the cause of equal treatment for women.

There are now women carpenters, electricians, boiler operators, and computer technicians. Even though macho male USAF and Navy pilots first grimaced when told that women would join their ranks, women are once again flying some of the world's fastest and largest aircraft. What's more, many of those same male "jet jockeys" who once disparaged females are now patting the accomplished new squadron members on the back and whispering "attaboys."

The modern-day armed forces have even relented to the extent that some, select women officers are at this moment isolated in silos deep beneath the earth where they literally hold the destiny of millions in their hands. These are the women assigned as Air Force missile launch officers for the Titan Missile System, the largest U.S. nuclear-tipped missiles.

In the horrible event that the President of the United States or other higher authority gives the word, these officers will receive a coded message in their facility which directs them to launch their awesome missiles—each of which has nuclear warheads with a destructive capacity equal to hundreds of atomic bombs the size of those which, in 1945, utterly destroyed the Japanese cities of Hiroshima and Nagasaki.

Some career military men have even trumpeted the previously unspeakable—that military women may actually be superior to men. For instance, Major General Charles Rogers, the Army's Chief of Personnel in Europe, asserted in an interview which appeared in *U.S. News & World Report* in April 1982, that, "Our female soldiers are better mentally than the men, and they're terrific competitors." A senior sergeant grudgingly agreed: "I'm basically a chauvinist," he said, "but in some ways they (women) are better than the men."

Said another male career serviceman: "A lot of women have established strong performance records. I'm proud to have them work with me."

Forget the Powder Puff

This fine work performance record has been compiled by women not only in office, clerical, and nursing jobs, but also in hard-core occupations requiring a minimum of powder and lipstick and a maximum of muscle power and perspiration.

Proudly, public affairs officers of the five services point out that today's servicewomen work in grimy work uniforms (called fatigues) doing dirty jobs like changing parts on jet engines and overhauling diesel generators.

Anyone for Heavy Vehicle Repairman?

A young female soldier we talked with at an army post in Texas provides an example of just how far the services have gone to accommodate women. Taking time off from her job as a heavy vehicle repairperson, she confided that she was pleasantly surprised at how well she had been accepted by her peers.

"They treat me like one of the guys," she said. "And I don't get any slack just because I'm a woman. But," she added, "they also know I'm one of the best damned mechanics assigned to the shop!"

The young woman told me that shortly after graduation from high school, she had sought employment at several civilian garages that repaired heavy vehicles.

"They laughed at me," she said. "One supervisor at a truck repair depot told me his insurance policy said 'No Women Mechanics'."

"At another garage, a snide employee winked and told me he wouldn't want to see me get my hands greasy."

This soldier's experience was far different when she joined the Army. The recruiter told her he was pleased to give her a job as a mechanic because "so many women recruits look for soft jobs—administration and so forth." She enlisted, was sent to a six-month technical school and assigned to her first permanent job.

"The first day on the job they told me I had to single-handedly break down and overhaul a fire truck engine. My superior, a sergeant who says I'm the first woman mechanic to work for him, didn't flinch when he gave me the assignment. He did watch over my shoulder to make sure I did the job right, but no more so than he does every new mechanic."

This able mechanic illustrates how successful many women have been once given the chance to show what they can do in a tough and demanding job area. This doesn't mean, of course, that a woman should not apply for a job in another, more traditional field of work. Society today is fast forgetting the rigid and unfair idea that some jobs are "women's work" and some aren't. The wise manager—both in civilian life and in the military—accepts a person for what he or she can contribute and not because of some preconceived notion of what work a woman should or shouldn't do.

So, if you are inclined to ask for a job as an administrative clerk or as a medical aide or whatever, then approach your military recruiter and seek that job. On the other hand, if your dream is to work in a job formerly labeled "for males only," go for that, too. It's your choice—except, that is, for those few jobs (about 12 percent of all those available) that are classified as combat. And maybe before long, you can ask for one of those jobs, as well.

The Job's Yours . . . Guaranteed!

The nice thing about military jobs and training is that all of the services will *guarantee* you a job and the training for it—in writing—*before you enlist.* That is, they will *if* you qualify for the job by a passing score on the military's entrance and placement exam—the ASVAB.

For example, if you want to be an administrative specialist, you have to score well on the portions of the exam which judge your reading comprehension and English composition.

Also, you may be administered a physical test by the recruiter for jobs that require heavy lifting of tools, equipment and supplies. This test, on a specially constructed digital measuring device, determines how many pounds you can safely and reasonably lift. Unfortunately, it has been shown that women have far less (about 58% less) lift strength in their upper torso than men, and this test often eliminates women from consideration for many jobs.

According to a study conducted by the Office of the Deputy Chief of Staff for Personnel, Department of the Army in November 1982, 132 of that branch's 351 job fields are rated in the very heavy category. This means that to win assignment to this field, an individual would have to be capable of lifting 100 pounds or more. The same study found that only about 7 percent of women soldiers had this strength capability, while a full 80 percent of the men qualified when tested.

The Army claims, however, that their test is gender-free, pointing out that both men and women are administered the same test. Thus, men also must meet the strength standard or face rejection for many career fields. It is wrong, they say, to mismatch a woman—or a man—to a job she or he can't physically accomplish.

Some critics may contend that the Army could manipulate the strength standard in a particular career field, simply to deny women the right to enter that job area. The service could, for example, claim a plumber must lift 100 pounds when 50 pounds is the correct figure. There's no proof that such manipulation is being done.

Job Areas Open to Women

Each service has defined which jobs are combat-related and which aren't. Those designated for combat are closed to women. Currently, here's how each of the services stand in regard to occupational areas open and closed to women: (Coast Guard figures not available)

Service	Total Jobs	Jobs Open to Women	Jobs Closed to Women
Army	354	293	61
Air Force	230	226	4
Marines	38	34	4
Navy	99	83	16
Totals	721	636	85

As you can see, women are excluded from quite a number of Army jobs (61 of 354, or about 17 percent) while the other services rate somewhat better in job opportunities.

The bright side of those statistics is that women may serve in the vast majority of military specialties. Overall, 88 percent of all occupations are open to women. Commendably, the Air Force has done the most to integrate women: 98 percent of its career areas are open to females.

Figure 3-1 shows the job distribution of U.S. military personnel. Note that only a minority of service members actually prepare for or can expect to see combat. Most are indirect participants—the backbone behind the fighters. For every combat, pilot, or infantryman, there are more than seven administrators, technicians, supply clerks, and similar support personnel.

JOB DISTRIBUTION OF U.S. MILITARY PERSONNEL

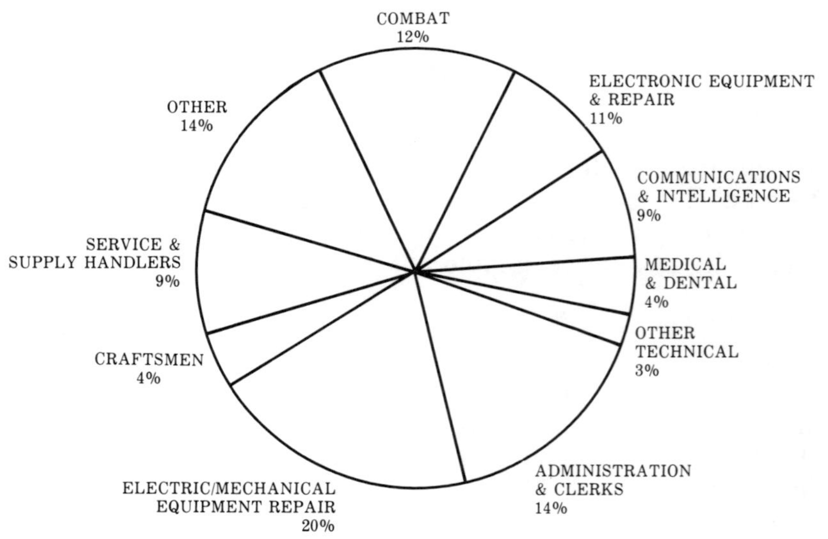

Figure 3-1
(Source: Department of Defense, 1984)

Enlisted Women in Hi-Tech Jobs

Modern warfare involves sophisticated weapons systems with advanced electronics, digital devices, and computerization. This, in turn, means that many of the enlisted jobs available are in high technology fields, like aviation, data processing, and electronics. This technical nature of military occupations is a prime attraction, and women have unlimited opportunities for these jobs. Maybe the Marines won't let you handle a weapon in combat, but you *can* be assigned to important positions in avionics and electronics maintenance. The Navy says "No" to women serving on submarines and combat ships. So, how about a hi-tech field like cryptologic technician? In this job, you'll be coding and decoding secret messages dispatched on highly sophisticated telecommunications equipment. Other positions, such as data processing technician, electronics technician, and engineering aide are also available.

It's been our experience that uniformed women in technical career fields enjoy very high status and prestige. In fact, we've received many complaints from ground soldiers and infantrymen—in combat skills—that the people in technical jobs get all the promotions or that they are favored and pampered just because the service has spent so much money in training them. Their complaints are well-founded. After all, it costs the Air Force about $100,000 to train just one computer programmer and the Navy the same amount to train a woman to repair aircraft electronic systems. Wouldn't *you* protect an investment like that?

Transferability to Civilian Jobs

The great thing about a hi-tech job is that if you later decide to leave the service, you'll be in a terrific position to land a high-paying, civilian job. You can hang up that uniform and start work almost immediately for IBM, Hewlett-Packard, McDonnell-Douglas, General Electric, or another firm in the market for workers with specialized training and experience in a technical field.

The military services recognize that their technically skilled people are in demand by civilian industry. For example, TSgt. Jim Hoffman, a career counselor at Bergstrom Air Force Base, near Austin, Texas, says that the Air Force typically has a serious shortage of people in hi-tech fields and a surplus of people in traditional fields like administration and supply. "People in the technical fields have highly marketable skills on the outside," comments Hoffman. "In some cases they can triple their salaries if they leave the service."

Training soldiers, airmen, and sailors for hi-tech fields is a costly proposition, so the services do their best to persuade these skilled workers to stay in and re-enlist once their initial term of service is completed. Often, the services offer huge re-enlistment bonuses for such people to sign-up for another term of three, four, or even six years. This bonus may be as high as $5,000 or $10,000. The top bonus payable is now $20,000.

Another sugar-coated lure to entice skilled technicians to stay in longer is the promise of assignment to the individual's base of choice. Say you are now in North Carolina, but want to transfer to California. Sign a re-enlistment contract and you'll soon be winging on your way to the sunny West Coast. On the other hand, there are those aerospace and computer corporations, also in California, that have offered you triple what you're getting from Uncle Sam.

Examples of Hi-Tech Career Fields

Here are just two examples in each service of the many hi-tech fields offered to women. In each of the fields listed the military service may have a number of different jobs.

AIR FORCE

Communications-Electronics Maintenance: Installs, modifies, maintains, and repairs television equipment, high speed data processing machines, automatic communications instruments, cryptographic/telegraphic equipment, and associated test instruments. **Comparable to civilian jobs of telecommunications technician and repairperson, radio/television and video systems technician, meteorological and teletype equipment repairer and installer.**

Intricate Equipment Maintenance: Overhauls and modifies photographic equipment. Works with fine precision tools, testing devices, and schematic drawings. **Comparable to civilian jobs of camera repairer, statistical and business machine and medical equipment repairer.**

ARMY

Electronic Warfare Intercept Systems Maintenance: Installs, operates, and repairs electronic intercept, measuring and testing equipment. **Comparable to civilian jobs of electrical instrument and meteorological equipment repairer and electronic equipment inspector.**

Aviation Communications-Electronic Systems Maintenance: Repairs and maintains navigation, flight control, ground approach radar, aerial surveillance and associated communications equipment. **Comparable to civilian jobs of aircraft electronics technician, electronic equipment repairer, radar repairer, and instrument mechanic.**

MARINE CORPS

Aircraft Maintenance: Repairs and maintains aircraft mechanical, electronic, and hydraulics systems. Also works on ground equipment used to support maintenance of aircraft. **Comparable to civilian jobs of aircraft mechanic, electrician, hydraulics specialist, machinist, sheet metal worker, aircraft instrument repairer.**

Data Systems: Computer operation and programming. **Comparable to civilian jobs of computer operator, computer programmer, and data automation controller.**

NAVY AND COAST GUARD

Air Traffic Controller: Controls air traffic, operates radar air control, uses radio and light signals, directs aircraft under visual and instrument flight conditions; assists in preparation of flight plans. **Comparable to civilian jobs of air traffic controller, airplane scheduler, and aircraft dispatch and log clerk.**

Ocean System Technician: Operates special electronics equipment to interpret and document oceanographic data. **Comparable to civilian jobs of computer-peripheral equipment operator, electronics technician, and oceanographic research assistant.**

As you can see from these few job descriptions, the military branches are well-endowed with hi-tech occupations for which you may apply. And don't let the technical sophistication of the descriptions frighten you. The service will fully train you even if you now know absolutely nothing about the job you will be doing once trained. Women who don't know the difference between AC and DC and know only that electricity is somehow connected with a wall outlet find themselves starting from scratch in a military technical school. Then, six months to a year later, they're at their first military base, working on incredibly complex computers and electronic equipment.

Of course, you may not be interested in a hi-tech field. Maybe you have your eye set on public relations, police work, intelligence, personnel, or those old standbys: administration and medicine. Fine, there's probably a job for you there, too. But just in case the promise of the information age and hi-tech era beckons, the military could be the place to start—and grow.

Landing the Job You Want

We mentioned earlier that to get the enlisted job you want, you will have to achieve an acceptable score on the Armed Services Vocational Aptitude Battery (ASVAB) test. Now let us explain further just how important this exam is and how you can do your best on it.

Every applicant for enlisted service takes the ASVAB. This exam tests your aptitude in a number of areas: general science, word knowledge, math, electronics, mechanical, and shop and automotive. Though the exam takes only 2½ hours to complete, its effects stay with you for your entire term in service. In fact, you have to attain at least a minimum acceptable score to even be eligible to enlist, and your score determines the jobs you can get and the training you'll receive to prepare for the job.

Prepare Yourself

Before tackling the ASVAB, make sure you are mentally and physically prepared. One suggestion is to obtain a copy of Barron's *How to Prepare for the Armed Forces Test* (ASVAB). This comprehensive book contains practice exams similar to the real thing and also includes tips on taking tests. Work all the practice test items in the book and review any areas where you need remedial help. Research studies have shown that persons who use an exam preparation book score appreciably higher (about 25 percent) on the ASVAB.

Armed with this practice, as well as a good night's sleep, you'll arrive at the exam site designated by your recruiter confident you are going to do well on the exam. And you will!

How the Services Use the ASVAB Results

The ASVAB is scored by computer, so almost immediately after you've taken the exam, a military job counselor of the service of your choice will have the results and be able to counsel you regarding the jobs for which your scores qualify. He will also have a list of jobs for which his service has an opening or *vacancy*. Consider that word *vacancy* carefully. For example, while the Army has a total of 293 jobs for women, not every job area will be available at the time you seek enlistment. Maybe only 150 of the job areas will have vacancies.

If There's No Vacancy

What do you do if your ASVAB scores are high enough for the job you want, but there's no vacancy? Three choices come to mind. First, you can simply choose another job that is available, perhaps in an occupational skill similar to the one that is your first preference. It is wise to have in mind at least three jobs (choices one, two, and three) at the time you talk to the military job counselor. Otherwise, you might end up making a hasty and unplanned decision which later you'll come to regret.

Another alternative is to check with one of the other services. Maybe another service will have a vacancy in your first choice of jobs and your ASVAB scores will meet that service's standards for the job. For example, let's say you want desperately to wear Air Force blue as a computer programmer, but the Air Force doesn't have a vacancy. Unless you're inseparably stuck on the Air Force, you can try the Army, Navy, Marines, or even the Coast Guard to see if one of those services has a computer programmer job for which you qualify.

A third alternative is for you to merely wait until there is a vacancy in the job of your choice in the service in which you plan to enlist. Unfortunately, you might have a long wait. Each service has a central computer at headquarters personnel that updates job offerings. The recruiting offices where the job counselors are assigned have remote computer terminals that receive this information. Maybe one day, the job you want will flash on their screen as "available." Then again, it may not.

The important thing for you to do is to *not become rushed.* Be mentally prepared every time you visit and talk with a recruiter or the military job counselor. Know what you want and exactly which alternatives are right for *you.* Don't become unduly alarmed by a recruiter who, after giving you the bad news that your first choice of jobs is not available, warns that "if you don't sign up today, even your second, third, or fourth choice of jobs may not be available tomorrow." Chances are these jobs *will* be available. Indeed, maybe tomorrow you'll hear the delightful news that the job you wanted most of all is now available.

Just remember: it's your life, not the recruiter's. Get the best deal you can. If you must accept a job that's not what you really wanted, at least understand why, and make that important choice on your own, at your pace.

Jobs for Women Officers

Up to now we haven't discussed the career fields open to women officer candidates. In most cases, these job opportunities parallel those for enlisted women. The difference is that officers typically are involved in the management and resarch aspects of jobs. Officers are the leaders and the supervisors. They are the engineers, executives, overseers, and advanced researchers. In the Navy and Air Force, they're also the only ones who navigate and pilot planes. In all the services, they serve as the commanders of units.

The officer jobs open to women can be both exciting and rewarding. Here's a partial list:

Accounting and Finance Officer
Missile Operations Officer
Space Systems Officer
Public Information Officer
Weather (or Meteorology) Officer
Scientific and Development Engineer
Computer Systems Analyst
Electronic Systems Officer
Administration Officer
Civil Engineer
Cartographic Officer
Aircraft Maintenance Officer
Transportation Officer
Supply Manager
Manpower Management Officer
Education and Training Officer
Management Analysis Officer
Military Police Officer
Criminal/Special Investigator
Health Services Administrator
Pharmacist
Physical Therapist
Clinical Social Worker
Flight Nurse
Veterinarian

There are many more jobs available for women officers than are listed here. The military recruiter of the service of your choice can provide you with a current list of jobs, along with a description of each. He can also advise you of the qualifications you'll need to meet eligibility requirements. Generally, your college major will be the determining factor in job assignment. For flying jobs, you will be required to attain an acceptable score on the section of an officer's candidate test that determines the individual's aptitude for flying aircraft.

All the Jobs for Enlisted Women: A List

The jobs or occupational areas open to women who enlist are listed below by service. The listings are alphabetical, except for the Air Force section which breaks down job titles by one of four broad fields: administrative, general, electronics, and mechanical. Also, the listings for Marine Corps and Coast Guard jobs are for career fields, rather than specific jobs or occupations. A career field is a broad occupational area that may encompass several, specific job specialties. For example, the Marine Corps' Data/Communications Maintenance career field includes such jobs (not listed below) as teletype technician, mobile data terminal technician, small missile systems technician, ground radar repairer, and microwave equipment repairer.

AIR FORCE

Mechanical Aptitude Area

Aerospace ground equipment mechanic
Air cargo specialist
Aircraft armament systems specialist
Aircrew egress systems mechanic
Aircraft environmental systems mechanic
Aircraft fuel systems mechanic
Aircraft loadmaster
Airframe repair specialist
Aircraft pneudraulic systems mechanic
Airlift/bombardment aircraft maintenance specialist
Cable and antenna installation and maintenance specialist
Construction equipment operator
Corrosion control specialist
Cyrogenic fluids production specialist
Electrical power production specialist
Environmental support specialist
Explosive ordnance disposal specialist
Fabrication and parachute specialist
General-purpose vehicle mechanic
Heating systems specialist
Helicopter mechanic
Jet engine mechanic
Liquid fuel systems maintenance specialist
Machinist

Marine engine specialist
Masonry specialist
Metal fabricating specialist
Metals processing specialist
Missile maintenance specialist
Munitions systems specialist
Pavements maintenance specialist
Plumbing specialist
Protective coating specialist
Reciprocating propulsion mechanic
Refrigeration and air-conditioning specialist
Seaman
Special vehicle mechanic
Tactical aircraft maintenance specialist
Turbo-prop propulsion mechanic
Vehicle body mechanic
Vehicle operator/dispatcher

Administrative Aptitude Area

Administration specialist
Airfield management specialist
Air passenger specialist
Chapel management specialist
Contracting specialist
Disbursement accounting specialist
Freight traffic specialist
General accounting specialist
Ground radio operator
Inventory management specialist
Morse systems operator
Operations system management specialist
Passenger and household goods specialist
Personal affairs specialist
Personnel specialist
Printer systems operator
Real estate cost management analysis specialist
Recreation services specialist

General Aptitude Area

Aeromedical specialist
Aerospace control and warning systems operator
Aerospace physiology specialist
Aircrew life support specialist
Air traffic control operator
Audiovisual media specialist
Club management specialist
Command and control specialist
Computer operator
Continuous photo-processing specialist
Dental assistant specialist
Dental laboratory specialist
Diet therapy specialist
Duplicating specialist
Education specialist
Electronic intelligence operations specialist
Entomologist
Environmental health specialist
Fire protection specialist
Food service specialist
Fuel specialist
Geodetic surveyor
Graphics specialist
Imagery interpreter specialist
In-flight refueling operator
Information specialist
Instrumentalist
Instrumentalist technician
Intelligence operations specialist
Law enforcement specialist
Maintenance analysis specialist
Materiel facilities specialist
Meatcutter
Medical administrative specialist
Medical laboratory specialist
Medical materiel specialist
Medical service specialist
Mental health clinic specialist
Mental health ward specialist
Motion picture camera specialist
Nondestructive inspection specialist
Occupational therapy specialist
Packaging specialist
Pharmacy specialist
Photolithography specialist
Physical therapy specialist
Printing-binding specialist
Programming specialist
Radio and TV broadcasting specialist

Radio communications analysis/security specialist
Radiologic specialist
Safety specialist
Site developer
Small arms specialist
Still photographic specialist
Survival training specialist
Target intelligence specialist
Telecommunications operations specialist
Veterinary specialist
Voice processing specialist

Electronics Aptitude Area
Aerospace photographic systems specialist
Airborne meterological/atmospheric research equipment specialist
Airborne warning and control radar specialist
Aircraft electrical systems specialist
Aircraft control and warning radar specialist
Air traffic control radar specialist
Analog flight simulator specialist
Analog navigation/tactics training devices specialist
Automatic flight control systems specialist
Automatic tracing radar specialist
Avionic communications specialist
Avionic inertial and radar navigation systems specialist
Avionic navigation systems specialist
Avionics aerospace ground equipment specialist
Avionic sensor systems specialist
Biomedical equipment maintenance specialist
Bomb-navigation systems mechanic
Defensive fire control systems mechanic
Defense systems trainer specialist
Digital flight simulator specialist
Electrician
Electric power line specialist
Electronic communications and cryptographic equipment systems specialist
Electronic computer systems specialist
Electronic-mechanical communications and cryptographic equipment systems specialist
Electronic switching systems specialist
Electronic warfare systems specialist
Ground radio communications equipment specialist
Instrumentation mechanic
Instrument trainer specialist
Integrated avionic communications, navigation, and penetration aids systems specialist
Integrated avionics attack control systems specialist
Integrated avionics component specialist
Integrated avionics computerized test station and component specialist
Integrated avionics elect warfare equipment and component specialist
Integrated avionics instrument flight control systems specialist
Integrated avionics manual test station and component specialist
Integrated avionics systems specialist
Missile control communications specialist
Missile electronic equipment specialist
Missile systems analyst specialist
Missile systems maintenance specialist
Missile trainer specialist
Missile warning and space surveillance sensor repair specialist
Navigational aids equipment specialist
Nuclear weapons specialist
Precision imagery and audiovisual media maintenance specialist
Precision measuring equipment specialist
Radio relay equipment specialist

Space communications systems equipment operator/specialist
Space systems equipment specialist
Telecommunications systems control specialist/attendant
Telecommunications systems equipment maintenance specialist
Telephone equipment installation and repair specialist
Telephone switching equipment specialist electro/mechanical
Television equipment specialist
Weapon control systems mechanic
Weather equipment specialist

ARMY

Accounting specialist
ADA operations and intelligence assistant
Administrative specialist
ADMSE repairer
ADP maintenance supervisor
Aerial sensor specialist
Aerial sensor specialist (OV-ID)
Aerial surveillance infrared repairer (Reserves only)
Aerial surveillance photographic equipment repairer (Reserve)
Aerial surveillance radar repairer (Reserves only)
Aerial surveillance sensor repairer
Airbrake repairer (Reserves only)
Aircraft components repair supervisor
Aircraft electrician
Aircraft fire control repairer
Aircraft maintenance senior sergeant
Aircraft pneudraulics repairer
Aircraft powerplant repairer
Aircraft powertrain repairer
Aircraft quality control supervisor
Aircraft structural repairer
Aircraft weapon systems repairer
Air defense radar repairer
Airplane repairer
Air traffic control (ATC) tower operator
Ammunition foreman
Ammunition inspector
Ammunition specialist
Animal care specialist
Antenna installer specialist
AN/TSQ-73 air defense
Artillery command and control system operator/repairer
Area intelligence specialist
Armament/fire control maintenance supervisor
Artillery repairer
ATC radar controller
Attack helicopter repairer
Audio/TV specialist
Audio-visual equipment repairer
Automatic data telecommunications center operator
AVIONIC communications equipment repairer
AVIONIC equipment maintenance supervisor
AVIONIC mechanic
AVIONIC navigation and flight control equipment repairer
AVIONIC special equipment repairer

Baritone or euphonium player
Bassoon player
Behavioral science specialist
Biological sciences assistant
Biomedical equipment specialist, advanced
Biomedical equipment specialist basic
Brass group leader
Broadcast journalist

Cable splicer
Calibration specialist
Card and tape writer (Reserve)
Cardiac specialist
Cartographer

Central office operations operator
Chapel activities specialist
CHAPPARRAL/REDEYE repairer
Chemical laboratory specialist
Clarinet player
Club manager
Combat area surveillance radar repairer
Combat telecommunications center operator
Communications-electronics maintenance chief
Communications-electronics operations chief
Computer/machine operator
Construction engineering supervisor
Construction equipment repairer
Construction equipment supervisor
Cornet or trumpet player
Correctional specialist
Counterintelligence agent
Court reporter

DAS 3 computer repairer
Data processing NCO
Defense acquisition radar mechanic
Dental laboratory specialist
Dental specialist
Dial/manual central office repairer
DSTE repairer

Electronic instrument repairer
Electronic switching systems repairer
Enlisted bandleader
ENT specialist
Environmental health specialist
Equal opportunity NCO
Equipment records and parts specialist
EW/Intercept systems repairer
EW/SIGINT analyst
EW/SIGINT chief
EW/SIGINT emitter identifier locator
EW/SIGINT morse interceptor
EW/SIGINT non-communications interceptor
EW/SIGINT non-morse interceptor
EW/SIGINT voice interceptor
Explosive ordnance disposal specialist
Eye specialist

Fabric repair specialist
Field artillery computer repair
Field artillery turret mechanic
Field general COMSEC repairer
Field radio repairer
Field systems COMSEC repairer
Finance senior sergeant
Finance specialist
Fire control instrument repairer
Firefighter
Fire support specialist
Fixed ciphony repairer
Fixed cryptographic equipment repairer
Fixed station radio repairer
Flight operations coordinator
Flute or piccolo player
Food service specialist
Forward area alerting radar repairer
French horn player
Fuel and electrical systems repairer
FV infantryman

General engineering supervisor
Graves registration specialist
Ground control approach radar repairer
Guitar player

Heavy lift helicopter repairer
Heavy wheel vehicle mechanic
HERCULES electronics mechanic
Hospital food service specialist

IBM 360 repairer
Illustrator
Image interpreter
Improved HAWK continuous wave radar repairer
Improved HAWK fire control mechanic
Improved HAWK firing control repairer
Improved HAWK firing section mechanic

Improved HAWK information coordination central mechanic
Improved HAWK launcher/mechanical systems repairer
Improved HAWK maintenance chief
Improved HAWK master mechanic
Improved HAWK pulse radar repairer
Improved TOW vehicle/infantry fighting vehicle/cavalry fighting vehicle system mechanic
Improved TOW vehicle/infantry fighting vehicle/cavalry fighting vehicle turret mechanic
Industrial gas production specialist (Reserve)
Intelligence analyst
Intelligence senior sergeant
Interrogator

Journalist

Land combat support system test specialist
Lance Repairer
Laundry and bath specialist
Legal clerk
Lifting and loading equipment operator
Light wheel vehicle/power generation repairer
Locomotive electrician (Reserves only)
Locomotive operator (Reserves only)
Locomotive repairer (Reserves only)

Machinist
MANSPADS crewman (man portable air defense system)
Marine hull repairer
Marine senior sergeant
Material storage and handling specialist
Material control and accounting specialist
Materials quality specialist
Mechanical maintenance supervisor
Medical laboratory specialist
Medical specialist
Medical supply specialist
Metal worker
Meteorological observer
Military police
Motion picture specialist
Motor transport operator
Multichannel communications equipment operator
M60A1/A3 tank systems mechanic
M60A1/A3 tank turret mechanic
M60A2 tank system mechanic
M60A2 tank turret mechanic

NCR 500 computer repairer
NIKE-HERCULES fire control mechanic
NIKE-HERCULES missile-launcher repairer
NIKE maintenance chief
NIKE test equipment repairer
NIKE track radar repairer
Nuclear medicine specialist
Nuclear weapons electronics specialist
Nuclear weapons maintenance specialist

Oboe player
Observation airplane repairer
Observation/scout helicopter repairer
Occupational therapy specialist
Office machine repairer
Operating room specialist
Operations central repairer
Optical laboratory specialist
Orthopedic specialist
Orthotic specialist

Parachute rigger
Patient administration specialist
Patient care specialist
PATRIOT missile mechanic
Percussion group leader
Percussion player
PERSHING electrical-mechanical repairer
PERSHING electronics material specialist
PERSHING electronics repairer
Personnel actions specialist
Personnel administration specialist

Personnel management specialist
Personnel records specialist
Personnel senior sergeant
Petroleum laboratory specialist
Petroleum supply specialist
Pharmacy specialist
Photo and layout specialist
Photolithographer
Physical activities specialist
Physical therapy specialist
Piano player
Power generation equipment repairer
Prime power production specialist
Programmer/analyst
Psychiatric specialist
Public affairs/audio-visual chief
Punch card machine repairer

Quartermaster and chemical equipment repairer

Radio operator
Radio teletype operator
Radio/television systems specialist
Railway car repairer (Reserves only)
Railway movement coordinator (Reserves only)
Railway section repairer (Reserves only)
Railway senior sergeant
Recruiter
Reenlistment NCO
Respiratory specialist

Satellite communications ground station equipment repairer
Saxophone player
Self-propelled field artillery system mechanic
Senior supply sergeant
SHILLELAGH repairer
SIGSEC analyst
Small arms repairer
Special agent
Special bandperson
Special electronic devices repairer
Station technical controller
Stenographer
Still photographic specialist
Strategic microwave systems repairer
Strategic satellite/microwave systems operator
Structures specialist
Subsistence supply specialist

Tactical circuit controller
Tactical communications systems operator/mechanic
Tactical microwave systems repairer
Tactical satellite/microwave systems operator
Tactical wire operations specialist
Tank turret repairer
Technical drafting specialist
Technical engineering supervisor
Teletypewriter repairer
Terminal operations coordinator
Topographic engineering supervisor
Topographic instrument repair specialist
Topographic surveyor
TOW/DRAGON repairer
Track vehicle mechanic
Track vehicle repairer
Traffic management coordinator
Train crewmember (Reserves only)
Transportation senior sergeant
Trombone player
Tuba player
TV/radio broadcast operations chief

Unit/supply specialist
UNIVAC 1004/1005 DCT 9000 system repairer
Utilities equipment repairer
Utility-helicopter repairer

Veterinary specialist
VULCAN repairer

Watercraft engineer
Watercraft operator
Water treatment and plumbing systems specialist
Weapons support radar repairer
Wheel vehicle repairer

Wire systems installer/operator
Woodwind group leader
XM-1 tank system mechanic
XM-1 tank turret mechanic
X-Ray specialist

COAST GUARD

Aviation Survival man
Aviation Anti-Submarine Warfare Technician
Aviation Electrician's Mate
Aviation Electronics Technician
Aviation Machinist's Mate
Aviation Structural Mechanic
Boatswain's Mate
Cryptologic Technician (Administrative)
Cryptologic Technician (Interpretive)
Cryptologic Technician (Maintenance)
Cryptologic Technician (Technical)
Dental Technician
Electronics Technician
Electrician's Mate
Fire Control Technician
Gunner's Mate
Hospital Corpsman
Damage Controlman
Photojournalist
Machinery Technician
Marine Science Technician
Musician
Radarman
Photojournalist
Quartermaster
Radioman
Sonar Technician
Storekeeper
Subsistence, Specialist
Telephone Technician
Yeoman

MARINE CORPS

Aircraft Maintenance
Airfield Services
Air Traffic and Enlisted Flight Crews/Air Support/Anti-Air Warfare
Ammunition and Explosive Ordnance Disposal
Auditing, Finance, and Accounting
Aviation Ordnance
Avionics
Band
Data/Communications Maintenance
Data Systems
Drafting, Surveying and Mapping
Electronics Maintenance
Engineer/Construction Equipment and Shore Party
Food Service
Intelligence
Legal Services
Logistics
Marine Corps Exchange and Clubs
Military Police and Corrections
Motor Transport
Nuclear, Biological and Chemical Warfare
Operational Communications
Ordnance
Personnel and Administration
Printing and Reproduction
Public Affairs
Signals Intelligence/Ground Electronic Warfare
Supply Administration and Operations
Training and Audio-visual Support
Transportation
Utilities
Weather Service

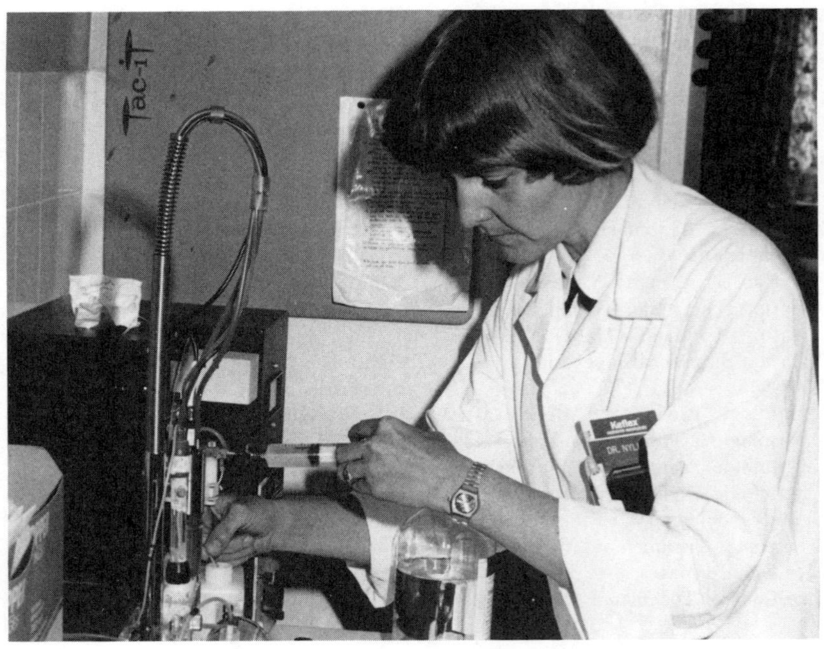

Major Barbara Nylund (Dr.) tests blood samples on a blood gas machine (U.S. Army).

NAVY

Aerographer's mate
Air traffic controller
Aircrew survival equipmentman
Aviation antisubmarine warfare operator
Aviation antisubmarine warfare technician
Aviation boatswain's mate
Aviation electrician's mate
Aviation fire control technician
Aviation machinist's mate
Aviation maintenance administrationman
Aviation ordnanceman
Aviation storekeeper
Aviation structural mechanic
Aviation support equipment technician
Boatswain's mate
Boiler technician
Builder
Construction electrician
Construction mechanic
Cryptologic technician, administration
Cryptologic technician, collection
Cryptologic technician, communications
Cryptologic technician, interpretive
Cryptologic technician, maintenance
Cryptologic technician, technical
Data processing technician
Data systems technician
Dental technician
Disbursing clerk
Electrician's mate
Electronics technician
Engineering aid
Engineman

Equipment operator
Fire control technician
Gas turbine systems technician
Gunner's mate
Hospital corpsman
Hull maintenance technician
Illustrator-draftsman
Instrument man
Intelligence specialist
Interior communications electrician
Journalist
Legalman
Lithographer
Machinery repairman
Machinist's mate
Master-at-arms
Mess management specialist
Mineman
Missile technicians
Molder
Musician
Navy counselor
Ocean systems technician
Operations specialist
Opticalman
Patternmaker
Personnelman
Photographer's mate
Postal clerk
Quartermaster
Radioman
Religious program specialist
Ship's serviceman
Signalman
Sonar technician
Steelworker
Storekeeper
Torpedoman's mate
Tradesman
Utilitiesman
Yeoman

Capt. Susan Rogers makes a preflight check on the wheel of her T-38 trainer (U.S. Air Force).

The Job Right For You

Well, how about it . . . after looking over this extensive list of military jobs open to women, have you come upon one or more that would be just right for you?

It has not always been the case that military women had their choice of so many worthwhile job specialties. The history of the armed forces reveals that it has only been in the last 15 years that job opportunities for women began to be more equitable with those available to men. Women have come a long way, yet there are a few remaining barriers to true equality for military women.

Comments from Military Women and Men

"They sent me to computer repair school, and I flunked out. It was easy but I partied and didn't study. What a dumbbell I was!"

—Pvt. Seymour Colson
Ft. Still, OK

"As a chaplain assistant, my job is unique. I'm like a civilian church administrator. I don't preach or lead the choir. I'm a professional, though, just like the chaplains."

A1C Linda Cramer
Lackland, TX

"I asked for an aircraft carrier. They gave me a submarine. I asked for electrician duty. I'm a mechanic. I'll admit a lot of people are more lucky, but me? Boy, have I had the shaft!"

—E-2, Navy
San Diego, CA

"Be sure to get a guarantee of that right job *before* you come in the service. Afterwards, it's too late. Be forewarned."

—TSgt., Air Force
Personnel Div., Lowry AFB, CO

"I think the Army is very fair in the way it assigns women to jobs. Because I scored high on the Army's entrance tests, I was given my choice of job I wanted. Then later, I volunteered for special training and got that, too.

—PFC Lydia Case-Smith
Ft. Knox, KY

"They said 'you're going to be a jeep driver' and I said no, I'm not! Well, I didn't quite say *no.* I sorta' asked for something more substantial. So they made me a personnel specialist. Sure beats a jeep!

—E-1, Army
Ft. Bragg, NC

"The Air Force sent me, after basic training, to a computer programming school for 48 weeks. Then, after another year, I was approved to go full-time for college and I will be an officer upon graduation. The opportunity is there if you go for it."

—Sgt. Patricia Allen
Wright-Patterson AFB, OH

"The Navy probably has more technical jobs than the Air Force, but most civilians think all we do is swab decks and paint ship hulls."

—Seaman George Lansing
Great Lakes, IL

"I'm a security policeman. I thought police work would be exciting. Now, I guard B-52's in the freezing, bitter cold. This isn't proper training for a job on the Detroit cop force, I'll tell you."

—A1C, Air Force
K.I. Sawyer AFB, MI

"I was a secretary in California and one day I joined the Air Force. So here I am—an F-15 (aircraft) grease monkey . . . I have no regrets."

—A1C Jeannie Campbell
Crew Chief, Kadena AB, Okinawa

"I came in the Air Force as a green second Lieutenant and was put into administrative work. How boring! I then applied for and became a weapons controller. I fly in an AWACS, get flight pay, and have a lot more fun. I have to say, though, that a lot of guys and gals prefer admin work. Not me!"

—Capt. Cathy Lardner
McCord AFB, WA

"I'm a prime example that the military does not know how to effectively use the talents that some of its members have to offer. It all started with my recruiter. I tried to get in a field related to photography, because I had two years civilian experience in a photo lab. However, after medical testing, my recruiter told me I had color blindness. He advised me to go into the intelligence field. Funny, I had my eyes retested and I'm not really color blind at all. Since I was gullible and ignorant at the time, I went with intelligence anyway. The most ridiculous thing about this is that I just won a photography contest."

—Sp 4 Russ Olson, Army
Ft. Leonard Wood, MO

"The many enlisted people working on the aircraft—the 'plane captains' are fantastic. When you are in the cockpit, you feel safe because you're betting your life they did their job."

—1st Lt. J. D. Nichols
Bombadier/Navigator, Cherry Point
NC Marine Station

You've Come a Long Way!

It was February, 1942, only a few months after the Japanese had surprised the world by bombing Pearl Harbor. The conversation in the cloakroom of the U.S. House of Representatives turned to the matter of a pending House Bill to establish a Women's Army Corps (WAC).

"I'll vote for it," said one young, progressive representative, "because every woman we put in uniform to sit in front of a typewriter will release one man for combat."

However, as he spoke, the look on the faces of his colleagues told the junior member of the Congress that his was an opinion not widely shared.

"Women in the military?" snarled one veteran Congressman. "In war time! Why that . . . that's preposterous!"

On the floor of the House, another member professed that he was astounded at the audacity of anyone who would even suggest womenfolk be allowed to don the khaki tans of the Army. According to Jeanne Holm in *Women In The Military,* the enraged Congressman said: "I think it is a reflection upon the courageous manhood of the country to pass a law inviting women to join the armed forces in order to win a battle. Take the women into the armed service, who will then do the cooking, the washing, the mending, the humble homey tasks to which every woman has devoted herself. Think of the humiliation! What has become of the manhood of America?"

Meanwhile, active duty military brass also voiced objections on the matter of women entering the nation's armed forces during the dangerous era that was World War II. Sneered one Navy admiral, "Sure, we'll take women on-board our ships. Anything to keep the morale of our sailors high." "Of course," he added suggestively, "only attractive young gals need apply."

The debate over this bill is an example of just where women stood in regard to military service in 1942, four decades ago.

Strangely, society failed to take into account the remarkable record of past women warriors. Overlooked was the outstanding performance of 13,000 women who served the military a quarter of a century earlier, in World War I.

The military services were a mirror of society, and society's feeling at the outbreak of the second World War was that a woman's place was at home. If she must work, the female should be in a protected office job or in some sort of social or volunteer church work.

But the armed forces? No, it just wasn't the custom of Americans to subject women to the rigors, discipline, and dangers of military life. That some women would, of their own volition, actually *choose* this way of life, and *seek* to join the armed forces was . . . well, it was to be disregarded.

However, the desperate need by the armed services for skilled non-combat personnel made the nation's elected leaders, and eventually the military brass, reconsider this hallowed custom. So a bill was drafted to permit large numbers of women to volunteer for military service. In another quote from Jeanne Holm, one Army colonel in 1941 lamented "We don't want women, but I guess we'll have to take them. We'd prefer dogs, ducks, or monkeys if we could use them."

"You're in the Army Now"

The colonel was right. The women *were* needed. The House Bill passed, over the objections of many military officers and conservative congressmen. The women's bill was also approved by the Senate and signed into law by the President. Soon, women volunteers were manning the ranks. During the next few years, the ranks of Army women swelled from a mere 939 in 1940 to a high of 163,644 in 1945. Over a hundred thousand more served in the other military branches. And these women served not only in front of typewriters or as "morale boosters" on combat ships, but in some of the more grueling and demanding jobs.

The new bill was designed so that women could, in fact, take on non-combat jobs and thus release men for combat, but Congress had not specified which jobs those were. The armed services quickly discovered that women were more than capable of handling jobs and tasks that, prior to that time, were considered nearly impossible for women to do. Women drove trucks, dug ditches, rigged parachutes, worked on machine tools, and even piloted airplanes during the war. Thousands served overseas and two were even taken prisoner-of-war by the Japanese. Many women were killed or injured by enemy action. Sixteen women won the Purple Heart, awarded to those wounded during war-time.

As for bravery, the Army Nurses Corps alone received 1,600 decorations, including Distinguished Service Medals, Silver Stars, Soldiers Medals, and Distinguished Flying Crosses.

Commenting on women's ability to withstand the rigors of war operations and of their impressive performance, according to Mattie B. Treadwell in *U.S. Army in World War II: Special Studies—The Women's Army Corps*, General Ira Eaker, Commander of the European Allied Air Forces, stated:

> "One of the factors in their success was courageousness. I saw this demonstrated when German planes came over . . . they keep more calm then the men in emergencies."

Women acquitted themselves so well during the war that an official Army study later concluded that "economical, efficient, and spirited results are achieved in military installations where both male and female personnel are on duty."

According to Treadwell, even Douglas MacArthur praised the women soldiers. Declaring women his "best soldiers," MacArthur remarked that military women worked much harder and were better disciplined than men—and they complained less."

"War's Over. Thanks . . . Goodbye!"

By war's end, on September 2, 1945, 265,000 women were serving in the Marines, Army, Navy, Coast Guard, and Army Air Corps (then part of the Army). They served admirably in a time of great national crisis. Unfortunately, once the emergency had passed, the nation felt that it was also time for the women to pass on from active military duty. Why? Well, according to Holm, Brigadier-General Gerald C. Thomas of the Marine Corps stated in October 1945:

> "Women have no proper place or function in the regular service in peacetime . . . The American tradition is that a woman's place is in the home."

It was ironic that after the war was over the contributions of American military women were so swiftly forgotten, for at the same time, some leaders of our defeated enemy, Hitler's Germany, were coming to the conclusion that if only *that nation* had used their womanpower, the outcome of the struggle may have been reversed. In a conversation with U.S. General Ira Eaker in 1976, Albert Speer, Nazi head of Germany's armament production stated:

> "How wise you were to bring your women into your military and into your labor force. Had we done that initially, as you did, it could well have affected the whole course of the war. We would have found out, as you did, that women were equally effective, and for some skills, superior to males."

Most Americans agreed that women had performed well, but the prevailing opinion was that ladies should serve *only* in war-time. So the women went home, honorable military discharges in hand. Within a few months, most women in uniform were separated from the service. Only the most talented and qualified women in hard-to-fill, critical job skills were retained by the services. Seemingly, women were no better off in 1945 than they were when the war had begun. Actually, this wasn't at all the case.

Women had gained something from their war experience. Because of their sterling performance and demonstrated ability to get the job done they had gained the admiration and respect of many of their male peers and superiors. Most important of all, the returning women veterans had earned for themselves a sense of purpose and a measure of self-respect and self-worth. No longer could men claim that women couldn't "hack it" in uniform. Men and women knew better.

Still, women veterans were faced in 1945 with a new situation. The emergency was over and they were being "invited" to turn in their uniforms and forget plans and thoughts of continued military service, or, perhaps, a career in the armed forces.

Displeased by this somewhat cold thanks for a job well-done, military women veterans let their elected leaders know of their displeasure. At the same time, the services slowly began to find the loss of many capable women a severe blow. Some military leaders, though a minority, even spoke up for a permanent and large women's group to be brought back on active duty.

Again, the War Call

Heeding these pleas, in 1948 Congress passed a law making permanent the inclusion of at least a small percentage of women to continue to serve in the military forces. Then, when the Korean War broke out, once again the call came for increased legions of women to help fill the ranks, and the numbers of women in uniform doubled.

However, after the Korean War, it happened again. The women were thanked, then escorted out the door, one-way ticket in hand for the passage home. Sufficient men could be found, claimed the generals and civilians in charge of our nation's defense, to man the military in peacetime.

Indeed they could: the military draft for men saw to that. During the 50s and early 60s, the draft hauled in all the men necessary to keep the services up to strength. Women could volunteer, but the services were limited by Congress to a total strength of no more than 2 percent women. In other words, for every 100 airmen, soldiers, sailors, or Marines, only *two* could be female: a token force.

The Vietnam Experience

The 2 percent rule for women came to an end in 1967. By that time, the Vietnam conflict had taken on menacing proportions and, once again, the nation began to eye women as potential military material.

As the Vietnam war raged on and the draft took its toll of eligible males, the 2 percent rule was abruptly abandoned and women volunteers were eagerly sought by the services. From 1967 to 1973 (at war's end) the female ranks increased in numbers at a fast pace, rising from 30,610 to 45,033 on active duty, an increase of almost 50 percent.

However, unlike World War II, when women were given the opportunity and proved themselves capable of handling jobs formerly reserved for males, during the Vietnam struggle, women were restricted primarily to that work defined as "women's work": clerical and administrative, and medical support positions. Said one military recruiter to an interested female recruit, "In the Army, you can be a typewriter soldier. We want you to stay a lady."

Evidently, many women didn't agree that ladies should only be found in the white medic uniform or at a typewriter. According to Major General Jeanne Holm, a respected Air Force officer and former Director of Women in the Air Force, morale of servicewomen during this period was at a very low ebb. Holm states that even though more women were brought onboard, their utilization was limited and their career prospects

These four members of a group of WASPS were trained to ferry the B-17 Fortresses (U.S. Air Force).

dim. Holm called it a period of "stagnation and regression."

This regression is very evident when one compared the numbers of women in the military in World War II with the totals on active duty in 1973. At the peak of the second World War, about 2.1 percent of those in uniform were women. Twenty-eight years later, at the height of the Vietnam War, the figure was only 1.9 percent. After almost three decades, women were worse off than before.

Progress Finally Comes

Even as things appeared bleak for women in 1973, changes were on the horizon that augured well for the future. Two major social movements had begun to take shape and each was to force dramatic changes for women, both in society as a whole and in the sub-culture that we know as our armed forces. These two great social advances were, first, the end of the draft and second, the burgeoning women's rights, or feminist, movement.

End of the Draft

When President Nixon ended the military draft in 1971, it was a definite plus for women. Without a draft to spur men to enlist and serve, the services were forced to turn to the huge numbers of women in society to help fill the projected gap in manpower. Suddenly, women were in demand and in a big way.

Kate Arbogast, a research economist with the George Washington University, noted this dramatic reversal in the fortunes of military women. Writing in *Military Review*, a professional service journal, Ms. Arbogast stated that: "Since the end of the draft the rate at which the services have been moving toward integration of women into their folds is astounding."

Arbogast stated that the most significant change took place in Fall, 1972, with most career fields being opened for the first time to women. This was followed up by sweeping new rules permitting women to participate in Reserve Officer Training Corps (ROTC) programs at colleges and universities.

However, Arbogast believes the end of the male draft was not the most significant factor in this newfound rediscovery of women as a military resource. Far more important was the emergence of a powerful women's rights movement which flowered in the late 60s and 70s, and resulted in the proposed Equal Rights Amendment (ERA).

The Women's Rights Movement

The women's rights movement in the United States began to take firm hold in 1972 with the passage by Congress of the proposed Equal Rights Amendment. Subsequently, the amendment was effectively killed as it was not passed by the necessary two-thirds of the state legislatures, a constitutional requirement. Yet, the impact of the proposed ERA on the progress of women in the military should not be underestimated.

The women's rights movement had first gained stature with the publishing of the book, *The Feminine Mystique*, by Germaine Greer, in 1962. Slowly, the forces of change took shape and the ERA became the spearhead in the overall movement for women's rights and for equality of opportunity. During the drive to ratify the proposed amendment, positive and far-reaching alterations began to take place in all of American society. The military was not immune to this rising tide of equality for women.

As the 70s progressed, the services threw out rule after rule that barred women from a full and equal role in our armed forces. Women made up a greater and greater percentage of the total number of personnel on active duty, and more and more occupational fields were opened to women. A real breakthrough came in 1976 when the service academies began admitting women. About the same time, the services moved to make their promotion systems more fair and equitable to women.

In 1969, the percentage of women in all branches of the Armed Forces was under 2 percent. In 1984, the Air Force led the way with women comprising 12 percent of the total personnel. Other branches are close to 10 percent, while the Marine Corps lags behind with only 5 percent.

Military Women Today—Have They Arrived?

Recently, I heard a service representative boasting that practically all barriers had fallen and that finally, women and men in uniform are equal—or nearly so.

Does this mean that everything is finally rosy for the military woman, that a utopia awaits those female citizens who choose the military way of life? Do our armed forces *truly* offer equal opportunity for women to serve—and to advance—within the military structure?

In summation, can a woman who today elects and enters the service be treated as a *person* and as a valuable human resource by her military superiors, regardless of her sex? The answer, regrettably, is . . . *no.*

Although military recruiters are loath to discuss this issue, and disgruntled males are too bitter to face up to it, the fact is that women face hurdles and obstacles in the military that men simply never find. Civilians at top leadership levels of the Defense Department recognize this inequitable and unfair state of affairs.

In 1982, Deputy Defense Secretary Frank Carlucci directed a series of memos to the service chiefs, directing the service chiefs to review their policies toward women and to remove institutional barriers that inhibit the full and effective use of women in the service.

Carlucci's boss, Secretary of Defense Caspar Weinberger, also has acted to break down institutional barriers that prevent the fullest use of military women. In a memo to all the services in late 1982, Weinberger told them to ensure that women were not subject to discrimination in recruiting or career opportunities. Weinberger admitted that, although the armed forces had "made much progress, some institutional barriers still exist."

Indeed they do. The *Air Force Times* in November, 1982, reported that the Defense Advisory Committee on Women in the Service (DACOWITS) found that the morale and outlook of military women was not good. Members of the committee, set up to advise the Secretary of Defense on women's matters, visited military bases the previous year and found "an underlying uneasiness among servicewomen about their perceived value to the military and the implied assumption that their presence denigrates readiness."

This uneasiness and poor morale among servicewomen has been noted by many Equal Opportunity officers—experts assigned at military installations to oversee the treatment of women, blacks, and other minorities. At a conference of these officers, held in Garmisch, Germany, in November, 1981, Dr. Sue Schlesinger, a research psychologist with the Army's Research Institute, stated that her study of military women assigned to Europe showed that:

- Due to stereotyping, women must work twice as hard for half the credit their male peers receive.
- Sexist/gender issues are eroding the morale of women *and* men.
- Gaining equality for servicewomen currently presents a bleak picture.

Our personal observation after discussing the status of women with hundreds of servicepeople—men and women—in researching for this book is that Dr. Schlesinger is at least partially correct. In comparison with men, women in the military are *not* at present given a fair shake.

Now before the reader concludes—wrongly, we believe—that the military is an ogre, an institution outmoded in its thinking and totally sexist in its actions, let us clarify this statement. As we said, the armed forces do, in fact, discriminate against women. However, it is only fair to say that this is a problem in all of society and not just within the military subculture.

Indeed, on close examination an objective observer can state that women have had—and now have—*even greater opportunities* in the military than in any single civilian industry, career field, or job specialty. A good case can even be made that the armed services have been and are today at the forefront in recognizing the legitimate career aspirations of working women.

It would be easy for us — or a critic of the military — to throw barbs at the services for their failure to fully integrate women into their framework. However, keeping things in perspective, the military is in many ways to be commended. There's still a way to go: women haven't fully arrrived — not yet. But, they're on their way!

WASPS Catherine M. Houser and Violet S. Wierzbicki stand by as Virginia Disbrow climbs into her Fairchild PT-19 prior to flight at Avenger Field, Sweetwater, Texas, May 1943 (U.S. Air Force).

Comments from Military Women and Men

"It might surprise some people but I haven't run into any prejudice from my fellow, Air Force ROTC male associates . . . everyone is given the same chance as officer cadets."

—Vickie Brown
AFROTC Cadet
Southern Illinois University

"To prove I am capable on a new job, I have to work at 150 percent. But it's not as bad as it was when I first joined the Navy. . . . I think that men are seeing that women can do jobs that used to be considered a man's job."

—PO/1C Cheryle L. Mills
USS Blakely

"I am sick of hearing about the battle of the sexes in the military. If a woman knew how to conduct herself as a military member and a lady, there would be fewer problems. . . . The one thing that bugs me is people insisting that (military) women be stripped of all feminine qualities."

—A1C Jessica J. Dailey
Utica, NY

"The last military exercise I went on was all-male except for myself. We slept in tents with C-rations to eat and no bathroom facilities. Instead of bemoaning my predicament, I put instincts and common sense to work to make that place as liveable as possible. . . . Thank God, all military women don't have the pampered 'Private Benjamin' outlook on life."

E-5, Army

"I started at the bottom . . . and received the chance to advance. Pride and professionalism help you go up the ladder. It doesn't matter if you're a man or a woman."

—Seaman (GM2) Mark Lansing
USS John F. Kennedy

"The military is color blind and sex blind. Anybody can be a success if they work hard. In civilian life it's who you know. If your uncle runs the company, you get promoted. In the service, no-one knows you from Adam! So the promotions go to the person who can convince his or her boss they are the best."

—SSgt. Jennifer Thornton
McConnell AFB, KS

"I was born in Amsterdam, immigrated to California when I was 8. I volunteered for the Netherlands when I joined the Air Force. I got my wish. I can speak the Dutch language and talk with the people here. When I tell them I am a jet mechanic, they are surprised—'You, a woman?' they remark."

—Jane G. Droogsma
Sr. Airman
Camp New Amsterdam, Netherlands

"I feel the military should bring back the draft—for women as well as men. The women demanding equal rights and opportunity deserve just that—the opportunity to lose an arm, leg, hand, scalp, . . . kill or be killed, sleep in the mud. . . . I welcome women in the service. Some are worth the salt of two men."

—E-6, Navy

"I have just returned to the States from Okinawa. Male marines treated us like dirt there. We could not walk out into the street without being verbally harassed. . . . Remember boys will be boys and that's what the military is all about."

Cpt. Janine Perrauh
Arlington, VA

"I handle millions of dollars worth of equipment. The Navy trusts me even though I'm only 21 years old. In the civilian work world, I'd be cooking up hamburgers at McDonald's. In the Navy, I'm somebody."

—PO2 Marcia Halstrom
San Diego, CA

"Any time men and women work together, there will be friction. But look around. Women are supervisors and officers in the Army. That's not true in a lot of civilian companies."

—Sgt. Roger Garvey
Ft. Bragg, NC

"I think women have it a little easier, but I don't blame it on the fact that their legs are softer than their male counterparts. . . . I think it's about time women started getting the respect they deserve and I personally think something should be done about the harassment they put up with."

HN A. J. Jones
U.S. Marines, Camp Geiger, NC

"A woman has to work twice as hard and keep one step ahead. It took me 6 months before most of the men would accept me as a coxswain (a person in charge of a small boat)."

—PO/2C Mary R. Laradie
USS L. Y. Spear

Bring Me Men! . . . And a Few Good Women

On the huge and imposing archway that towers over the campus of the Air Force Academy in Colorado Springs, Colorado, is sculpted the following bold, but simple, pronouncement: BRING ME MEN! The words were placed there at the time the Academy complex was constructed, back in the 50s.

Things have changed a great deal since 1959, when the Air Force Academy opened its doors to its first class of promising, new male cadets. Perhaps the most important—even revolutionary change—has been the introduction of women cadets in 1976. Still, the words BRING ME MEN! continue to command the attention of cadets, faculty, and visitors alike as they go to and fro on the grounds of this beautiful campus.

Perhaps it is fitting that this inscription stay as it is for now because its words are by no means entirely passé , nor is the message of the inscription a nostalgic symbol of times past—a throwback to a bygone era when male warriors ruled supreme. The marching order given military recruiters by their superiors has over the years remained a constant one: BRING ME MEN!

However, we can't help but tell of the witty woman sergeant at the Academy who wryly quipped that the words, "Oh, yes, and a few good women, too!" should be added to that seemingly eternal, but antiquated phrase.

The good sergeant's comments were right on target: the services *are* looking for a few good women. The operative words here are *few* and *good.* This is in contrast to the expensive (a billion dollars annually!) talent search and head hunt conducted by recruiters for eligible male recruits: *many* men are needed and the services will take a man over a woman even if he's *not* quite as good nor nearly as well-qualified.

This inequity in recruiting is not the only roadblock faced by women. There are numerous spheres of service life where servicewomen today are not being treated equally or where their career opportunities are limited in comparison to those for men. In addition to recruiting, other areas of discrimination are: job assignment, promotions (career advancement), and geographical assignment. In addition, many military women today believe that sexual harassment is a major problem.

Inequity #1: Recruiting

The friendly military recruiter's office is the first step for a woman interested in uniformed service. It's also the most important, because it's at this juncture that is determined:

- If you are eligible to join the *service* of your choice.
- The *career fields* for which you are qualified.
- The type and extent of *training* you'll receive.
- The military base or installation to which you'll be first *assigned.*

In other words, if you want that dream job, in the service you most admire, at the site or location where you most want to go, it's the military recruiting personnel who can get you winging on your way. On the other hand, it's also the experienced career sergeants and enlisted persons at the Recruiting Service who just may be the bearer of bad news: that you're *not* going to get what you want in regard to service, job, training, and geographical location.

Given that this first step in a woman's service career is of such ultimate significance, it is sad to report that, at the recruiting office, female recruits are not nearly as welcome as males.

Only a limited number of women are allowed to enlist. Women also must meet higher standards for enlistment then men in the areas of entrance exam scores and education level.

Before you start screaming at how unfair the military's recruiters are, let us hasten to say that this unfair situation isn't entirely of their doing.

The primary reason that women applicants aren't as desirable to a recruiter as men is that the military simply doesn't *need* as many women as it does males. Congress dictates how many women may annually enter the services and that body has set exact limits on how many women recruiters can enlist.

For example, as of 1984, the Army was limited to slightly more than 65,000 enlisted women, or about 9.6 percent of the total number of soldiers on active duty. This is the maximum allowable, and the Army can enlist more women only when women now in uniform either die or are discharged. If, say, 5,000 women depart the Army ranks in a given year, Army recruiters may enlist exactly that many recruits to replace them—thus bringing the 65,000 figure back to full strength.

The other services have limits as well: for the Air Force, only 12 percent of the enlisted force may be women; the Navy has a much lower limit of 7.8 percent. The Marines apparently are the least open—some would say hostile—to women: only 4.4 percent of Marine Corps active duty personnel are female. That's less than one out of 20!

These percentages work out to the following numbers. This is the total number of enlisted women on active duty in each of the armed services as compared to the total number of personnel, both male and female:

Service	**Women**	**Total (men and women)**
Army	65,167	674,494
Navy	37,051	476,894
Marines	7,748	174,806
Air Force	54,562	477,091

It's obvious that a woman will have a more difficult time enlisting in the Army—or in any of the five services—than would a man. Is this fair? Well . . . no. Demographic studies indicate that 50.6 percent of the people in the enlistment age group are female—that's *over half* the entire population eligible for military service. Yet, as it stands today, women comprise only 9 percent of those in uniform. And the services cannot bring in more women: Congress forbids it.

Defense officials say that things will get better over the next five to 10 years. The DOD now projects that, by 1990, women will constitute about 11 percent of those in our armed forces. But this means the current discriminatory system will be only slightly improved and men will continue to have far greater opportunities to enlist. If the DOD's 1990 targets for women are reached, there will still be 9 men for every one woman on active duty.

Civilian Comparison

The military's figure of 9 percent women—11 percent projected for 1990—is not at all a glowing one when compared to the progress being made in civilian professions and occupations. In many areas our armed forces have been at the vanguard in insuring the rights of women, but sheer numbers is not one of those areas.

While military personnel officers boast of the gains made by women in the past decade and point out that 9 percent is a vast improvement, Labor Department statistics show that the civilian work world has done as well or better in accepting women. As of 1981, 19 percent of the doctors and dentists were female, and women accounted for 14 percent of the lawyers and judges. Women became the majority in such fields as insurance adjustor and real estate agents, and they constituted 21 percent of the blue collar work force.

Clearly, utilization of women by the armed forces has a long way to go. As Shirley Bach and Martin Binkin have pointed out in a Brookings Institution study, "Present laws and policies deny women their full rights and deny the nation a pool of competent workers."

The Unavoidable Recruiting Quota

As a result of this imbalance in the ratio of women eligible to enlist, recruiters are often told to discourage women from enlisting. Formally, this comes in the form of lower recruiting quotas for women. If, for example, a recruiter in Dallas or in San Diego has a quota in a particular month of 50 men and only 5 women, he quite naturally will be pleased when a male applicant walks in the door. He may also be receptive to a woman but, in the end, it's the male who is his most needed and desirable customer.

In some cases, a recruiter may not be given a female quota at all. If he does then enlist a woman, he will receive no credit toward meeting the overall quota. If this recruiter is hard put to fill his all-male quota and he's far behind in his recruiting efforts, it's apparent that any woman who approaches him will be given only the minimum of advice and consideration. After all, everything the recruiter does to assist a woman applicant is time taken away from his efforts in meeting that cursed, all-male quota.

Women, then, become a bother. The recruiter's job and career advancement is on the line. "Men first," the poor, bedraggled recruiter may exclaim, and understandably so, for that's exactly what his superiors have in mind.

Aviation Structural Mechanic Airman makes pre-flight checks of a helicopter (Naval Photographic Center).

ASVAB and Education Level

This inequity is compounded when we consider other obstacles encountered by women who seek to enlist. For one thing, women may be required to attain a higher score than men on the armed forces entrance exam. For another, the service may demand that a woman have attained a higher education level.

As of January, 1984, all the services require women to possess either a high school diploma or the equivalent (GED test certification). Men who score high enough on the ASVAB need not have a diploma. Thus, in the most recent recruiting year, 69,160 male, non-high school graduates enlisted—19 percent of all enlistees. Not a single woman was granted this privilege.

As for the scores required of women on the ASVAB, here are current minimum standards for the services. Note that women must score nearly 67 percent higher than men to join the Marines and three times as high as men to meet the Army's minimum acceptable ASVAB score.

Service	**Minimum Acceptable ASVAB Score**	
	Men	**Women**
Army	16	50
Air Force	21	21
Navy	31	31
Marines	31	50
Coast Guard	31	31

It's obvious that men find it easier to enlist than women. It's also obvious that servicewomen, on the whole, are far sharper mentally than their counterparts. Since only 9 percent of all military personnel can be women, the recruiters can afford to be choosy in selecting women for enlistment. There are many qualified applicants vying for the few female slots.

The question, of course, is why this 9 percent restriction? Why has Congress decreed this? The answer, put succintly, is that unlike men, women may not be assigned combat jobs.

Inequity #2: Job Assignments

Women are prohibited by law from assignment to Navy, Air Force, Marine and Coast Guard jobs in which they may be involved in direct combat. The Army enforces this same rule by regulation. Thus, women can't work on combat ships (almost *all* ships are designated as combat), aircraft carriers and submarines, they can't fly bomber aircraft, and they can't be given a job in tanks or infantry.

As the very mission of our armed forces is combat—that of fighting and winning battles—this combat restriction is a serious drawback for women. Not only are women excluded from career fields and jobs that are in the combat category, but the services also must be sensitive about *where* women may be sent.

If a crisis or conflict breaks out in Africa or the Middle East that requires the military to intervene, it's likely that women will be left behind. Later, after the battlelines are drawn, women in uniform *may* be brought over—to assist behind the lines in non-combat, or support, functions.

An Unwise and Impossible Policy

Many experts contend, however, that trying to keep women away from the battlefront is not only *unwise*, it's impossible. It's unwise, they say, because if a unit must hastily mobilize and leave by aircraft or ship for a world troublespot, gaping holes in manpower would result because of the skilled women servicemembers who are left behind. The shorthanded units would be far less ready for combat, as some men would be doing not only regular combat roles, but filling in for the missing women.

Also, if a major war occurs, it will be impossible to restrict women from the shooting and killing because who can predict *where* the battleground will be? For example, tens of thousands of servicewomen now stationed in Western Europe will immediately find themselves in the thick of battle if the Soviet Union were to attack. NATO studies warn that the Soviet armies could possibly roll over the entire continent in a matter of weeks. It's ludicrous to assume that women will be spared combat.

As the communist forces advance, all talk of excluding women from the fighting would dissolve into one primary directive: Let's use *everyone* we have to prevent defeat and insure victory. It will likely be kill or be killed—and sex be damned!

Regardless of the wisdom and the practicality of the no-combat policy, the military services blithely accept the status quo and continue to operate under the fiction both that women can be isolated from battle and that their absence would not detract from combat-effectiveness.

Regrettably, the exclusion of women from combat inevitably makes women second-class citizens in the military. It's hard for women to claim for themselves equal status and comparable rights to promotion, career advancement, and even pay, when it's only the men who hazard their lives in battle.

As Helen Rogan, author of *Mixed Company,* found after a unique and intensive two-week study of women Army soldiers undergoing boot camp training, life in the Army is overlaid with "combat mystique." A caste system exists—an artificial division between combat and non-combat soldiers. The fighters have the high status and aura of leadership; the support troops are relegated to the "seconds" bin. We can testify personally that this same situation exists in all the branches of service.

Some women may be happy with this situation. Not everyone is eager to put their lives on the line and some women may feel comfortable being relegated to support and "behind the battle lines" jobs. But a good number of women find this restriction a career detriment, and their complaints are becoming increasingly vocal.

One military woman we talked with bitterly told us that keeping a servicewoman away from combat was like keeping an Exxon employee away from oil and gas, and a General Motors assembly line worker away from autos. "In either instance," she explained, "the employee's career would be effectively destroyed before it had begun."

A few senior Defense Department officials have admitted to a severe liability that women face because of this combat restriction, but they contend the same holds true for men in non-combat specialties. Secretary of the Navy John Lehman, in 1982, commented that "there is no question that women—and men—without warfare specialties are at a disadvantage." The Navy Secretary failed to mention that men, at least, have a shot at combat jobs. Women don't.

Should Women Fight?

The issue of women in combat can be a very emotional issue and there are those who believe that women lack the killer instinct. "I can't see a woman slitting an enemy's throat," was how one grizzled Marine colonel put it.

His was a graphic way to put the issue—and an unfair, skewed way also. The technological nature of war in our modern era is such that in any major war between the United States and an enemy, death would inevitably be a long distance affair. Neutron weapons, chemical-biological armaments, laser "death rays," air-to-air rockets and anti-tank missiles, and dozens of other sophisticated weapons have practically made hand-to-hand combat obsolete.

Our estimate, backed up by other experts, is that no more than a miniscule one or two percent of military personnel would, in a future armed conflict, need the old-fashioned, "mud, blood, and guts" fighting skills. Even then, it seems to me that there are at least a few women in America today who have the muscle and brawn and the predisposition and soldierly attitude necessary for close combat. Yet, the rule is now—applicable to all women—"No Fighting, Ladies."

Inequity #3: Promotion Opportunity

The services are prone to claim that women have full and equal opportunity for promotion and career advancement. Theoretically, they're correct. The same promotion standards are used to promote men and women. In each service there is only one uniform promotion system for all. Nevertheless, in at least two ways, women are at a disadvantage.

First is that old bugaboo—the combat restriction. The very essence of the military tradition—the sole reason for existence of an armed force—is the readiness to wage war, wherever and whenever called upon by the nation. Naturally, the lion's share of promotions goes to the personnel who most directly contribute to this important mission. Only men go to war so only men have the advantage of developing a military combat record that will enhance ultimate promotion opportunity.

It's true that we now have women in the higher ranks—even a few generals and admirals. Some women command large numbers of men and otherwise exercise significant responsibilities. This book will introduce a few of these women in a later chapter.

However, it is an indisputable fact that women have a tough time in overcoming the no combat stigma. All the services reserve their top positions for men who have demonstrated their ability to function in a combat environment. This includes men who have first proven themselves to be able pilots, infantry commanders, combat ship officers, and so forth.

The proof of this is in the data provided the authors recently by the Department of Defense. Consider:

- Of the 25,095 women officers, 21,287—84 percent—serve in the lowest three pay grades. This compares to only 64 percent of the men officers serving in these grades.
- Of 1,174 generals and admirals on active duty, only 6 are women, an insignificant .5 percent. Half of these are in the nursing field. Incidentally, the Marines have *no* women generals.

No matter how talented and capable, no woman can present the necessary combat credentials for high-level promotions. The few "star" officers—the women generals and admirals—are assigned administrative-type duties in functions like personnel, scientific research, training, education, and services—non-combat roles. As one woman officer interviewed told us, "We're likely to see a woman president before we'll see a woman on the Joint Chiefs of Staff."

The Sunny Side of Things

However, all is not bleak. While women do face insurmountable odds in winning promotion to star-rank, there are only a small number of generals and admirals in the armed forces anyway. Only those career men (plus a few select women) who demonstrate the ultimate in leadership over a period of over twenty years have the slimmest chance to earn such a high rank.

There are plenty of other advanced positions to shoot for—from corporal or airman first class to master sergeant and on up to colonel. 99 percent of the people in uniform are in these ranks, and generally, promotions are based on how well you do your job, not on your sexual gender.

As you move up the ranks as a career military person, it does become progressively harder for women to be promoted on an equal basis. But in the lower ranks and during your first ten years or so in uniform, your chances as a woman are as good as a man's—even if he's in a so-called combat job. As a matter of fact, your promotion opportunity as a woman is *bet-*

Capt. Stella Sellers is an Army Chaplain at Hunter Post Chapel, Ft. Stewart, Georgia (U.S. Army).

ter than that of a man. Figure 5-1 lists the average time a person had spent in service when he or she was promoted to the rank shown (E-grades are used by all the services to denote pay grade). Note that in every enlisted grade, women had less time in the military than men when promoted. According to the Department of Defense, one explanation is that enlisted women in most grades are better educated than their male counterparts. A second explanation is that enlisted women are performing better than men.

AVERAGE TIME IN SERVICE WHEN PROMOTED

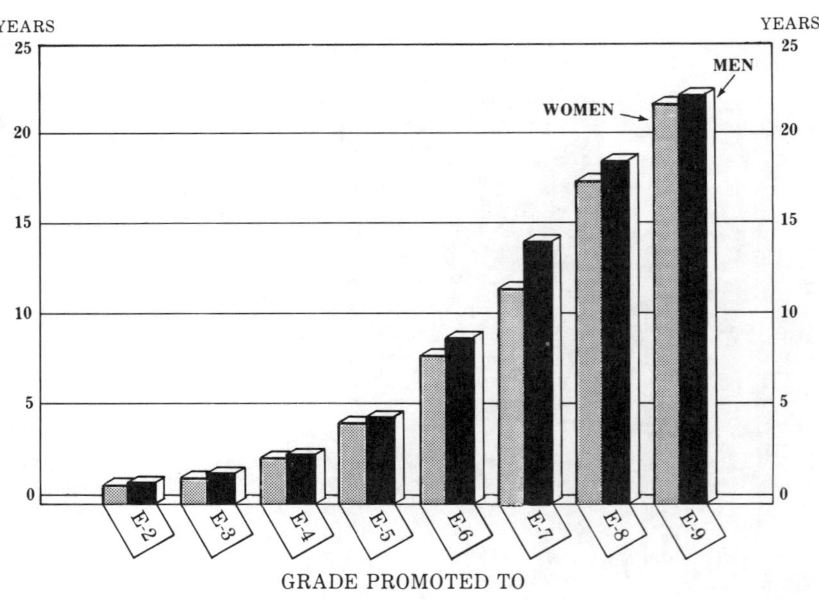

Figure 5-1

Men Have Support Jobs, Too

For those women who are worried that the no-combat rule discriminates only against women, it is important to realize that the majority of men are in support, rather than combat jobs. Contrary to what civilians mistakenly believe, *most* military jobs are support.

For every infantryman, there are seven people in occupations such as cook, driver, personnel, mechanic, computers, supply and finance. All these people are mission-essential. But like their female colleagues, men in support positions often find that the door is closed to their advancement to the uppermost echelons of the military hierarchy.

Pay Equality and Comparable Worth

Also, in fairness to the military, it should be mentioned that women in the armed forces are not subject to two forms of job discrimination commonly found in civilian life. The first concerns the issue of pay for jobs of comparable worth; the second is the inequality of pay between men and women in identical jobs.

The comparable worth issue involves the paying of personnel in a traditional women's field less than the salary paid to men in a traditionally male career field. For instance, secretaries and nurses may be paid less than the janitors and kitchen aides who work at a hospital. Why? Simply because the secretarial and nursing fields are predominantly made up of women. Thus, employers pay less, though the workers' contributions may be comparable or even greater in the traditional women's field.

The inequality of pay between men and women in an identical field is also a problem in civilian jobs. Discrimination occurs when, for example, a woman manager is paid less in salary than a male manager of comparable status and position. It also may occur when a female plumber, computer operator, or policeman is paid less by an employer than a male performing in the exact same job.

These forms of discrimination are commonplace in civilian work. As Thelma Kandel states in her book, *What Women Earn:*

> "Despite great strides made by working women over the past decade . . . One out of ten female workers earn as much as males in similar jobs . . . male high school dropouts earn as much as $1,600 more (annually) than female college graduates."

The good news for military women: things are different in the armed forces. People are paid by their rank (their military E-grade) and their seniority and not according to the caprice of Uncle Sam, their employer.

Thus, in the Army, E-3 carpenters with 2 years experience—male and female—are paid exactly the same; two USAF captains, male and female, who pilot C-130 cargo planes receive equal pay; and two Marine E-7 office managers—one male and one female—draw the same salary. Identical pay for identical jobs. There is only one pay scale, and gender has no bearing whatsoever.

Not only that, but the matter of comparable worth is resolved by the military's pay method. E-5 cooks, E-5 computer programmers, and E-5 administrative clerks receive equal pay. All persons of the same military grade and years of service are paid exactly the same regardless of career field or job specialty, or sex. The military thinking is that an airman is an airman, or a sailor is a sailor: *all jobs* contribute to mission-success.

For example, combat soldiers can't fight unless they eat, so who says the cook isn't just as essential as the foot soldier? The issue of a field being women's work is not even considered. There's no such thing.

Labor unions, workers' federations, and women's rights groups are raising cain throughout the nation because of the inequities in pay and compensation prevalent throughout society. Perhaps they should look to the military as a model for the civilian work world. Pay equity is simply not one of the inequalities of service life.

Who Do You Know?

Another negative feature of many civilian jobs is that promotion and career advancement is so often based on "who you know" rather than on how well you do your job. If a person's dad, uncle, or brother happen to be head of the firm, then obviously that individual has a royal road to advancement within the firm. Not so in the military. We're all related to Uncle Sam!

Everyone starts off the same in the armed forces. We assure you your training instructor at boot camp really could care less if your dad's name is Rockefeller or your uncle is head of IBM. Once on the job, everyone wears the same uniform. The military bureaucracy is the great leveler.

In fact, in the lower enlisted ranks in the Air Force and Navy, most promotions are based on how well a *computer* ranks you in competition with your peers. In the Navy, personnel are promoted to a large extent on how well they score on computer-graded job exams.

The Air Force also tests its enlisted people on their job knowledge as well as on general military subjects. Then the scores are combined with other, objective factors such as time in grade and service and the numerical grade given a woman on her supervisor's written performance report. The overall results, judged by computer, determine who will be promoted. There are no promotion boards for most military grades and no single individual to pick a favorite.

All in all, the services probably provide a more equitable and merit-based system for selecting personnel for promotion than do the vast majority of civilian organizations. There are inequities, as we have discussed, and these need attention. But the positive elements also deserve to be recognized.

Inequity #4: Geographical Assignment

Another area of discrimination for women is in geographical assignment. This is no longer a major concern, but there still exist a few military installations where women are barred from assignment. Sometimes it is due to the lack of separate facilities for women at a military site. For example, the Air

Force doesn't assign women to its Minuteman Missile sites as missile officers because the silo capsules accommodate only men.

There is, however, another, even more unfair reason why women are not assigned to Minuteman Missile jobs. USAF studies have shown that the majority of wives of missile officers object to the assignment of women. The wives complain that another woman would be all alone in the capsule with *their* husbands, for hours at a time.

Navy men told us that their wives would also be opposed to women being assigned on ships with their husbands. Again, the wives fear that "something" may happen because of the close accommodations on board vessels and the fact that the ships are out at sea for so long.

One problem the services have confronted in assigning women is the reluctance of a few nations—mostly in the Moslem world—to accept U.S. military women. In Saudi

Private Laura Lozano operates an ARMY HAWK Missile loader/transporter (U.S. Army).

Arabia and some other countries, women are segregated and it is contrary to custom and tradition for women to serve in the military. In an effort to foster good relations and practice tolerance, the U.S. does not assign women to such nations.

Could this, one may ask, be considered as bowing to the prejudice of the foreign nation concerned? The answer can only be yes, but then, the services point out that it is *their* country and we are invited guests. The services neglect, however, to add that the American military often is a *paying* guest.

Sexual Harassment

One of the most volatile issues in the continuing adjustment of the services to women is that of sexual harassment. Some contend that the military is a seething hotbed of sexual harassment of the military women.

Actually, this issue is not peculiar to the military, but is also a hot potato in the civilian workworld. Wherever women are subordinate to male superiors, there arises the danger, however slight, of sexual harassment.

In the armed forces, there is strict adherence to the doctrine of obedience to orders and much attention is paid to the dictates and suggestions of superiors. Therefore, the opportunity for a male military supervisor to harass a woman subordinate is probably greater than in civilian industry.

Fortunately, unlike the hopeless situation some women encounter in the civilian workworld, women in the military have recourse when male superiors attempt to extort sexual favors. Women are encouraged by service regulations to report superiors who harass. This harassment can take on any or all of the following manifestations: physical patting of sensitive body areas, use of suggestive language, an implication that sexual favors may be repaid by some advantage, or a demand for "sex or else." No matter what form the harassment may take, such behavior is frowned upon harshly by the armed services.

One service recently issued a memorandum that told commanders they should "act quickly to eliminate the discriminatory act and impose proper sanctions against the offender including a court-martial if indicated."

The other services have issued similar directives to prevent sexual harassment and punish offenders. General Lew Allen, Jr., Chief of Staff USAF, stated bluntly:

> "People who engage in such practices violate professional standards, human dignity, and also diminish mission effectiveness."

Our experience has been that these directives are being followed. There are exceptions and if a military woman believes she is the victim of sexual harassment, she may report this to either a superior or officer higher up in the chain of command. She may also report the incident to her first sergeant or commanding officer, to the base or post equal opportunity officer, or to the inspector-general (IG). Every military installation has an equal opportunity officer who is empowered to investigate complaints of wrongdoing. The IG of an installation can, if necessary, cut through red tape and the bureaucracy to redress misconduct.

Women have so many avenues to complain and service regulations are so definite on this matter, that sexual harassment is nowhere near the problem that it is in the civilian world. But, however subtle, it does still exist.

Invariably, the military will act to correct the situations where women are mistreated. But if it doesn't, the servicewoman can write her Congressman and describe the situation. He can then initiate an investigation by asking the Pentagon to look into the allegation.

The Scorecard

It's apparent that in our armed forces women are not yet quite equal to men. The most serious and damaging inequities are found in the recruiting process and in the job restrictions applied to female recruits. Lesser problems—although ones that demand attention and correction—are the limitations on where women may be assigned and the continuing instances of sexual harassment.

These are areas of discrimination that are not easily amenable to treatment, at least not in the short run. In terms of the combat issue, America has not yet decided just how far it wants to go in fully integrating women into its armed forces. Controversy still rages as to whether the combat restriction for women should be lifted and women trained to meet and kill our enemy—and perhaps be killed.

One thing is for sure. Once society does make up its mind, and our national leaders give the signal, our military can be expected to pitch in and make things work. The many men and women in uniform are dedicated people with the best interests of our country at heart. They'll follow the guidelines set down by society and they'll continue to defend us, come hell, high water—or the enemy.

Quartermaster 2nd Class Linda Coffelt plots a chart in the pilot house of the repair ship USS Vulcan (Naval Photographic Center).

How the Inequities Affect You

There's no doubt that women are a valuable asset to the armed forces. So if you really want to join the service, don't let the inequities hold you back. Sign-up, show the military how valuable you are, and, if you're so inclined, fight to gain full equality for military women.

If you choose the military, your first inequity will be encountered immediately, at your recruiter's office. The recruiting system is definitely *not* designed to promote the acquisition of women into the armed forces. Still, each year thousands of women do successfully navigate the hurdles met at the recruiting office. Don't be discouraged. If you've got what it takes, you can too. You might even run into a friendly and positive recruiter who has a healthy respect for the abilities and the contributions of military women. Quite a few recruiters do.

After you're on active duty and doing your best to prove your ability and dedication, you'll find that many active duty personnel will appreciate your efforts. You'll also find that, regardless of the inequities, our armed forces offer many advantages to women who qualify and who are willing to serve.

Comments from Military Women and Men

"My big bitch is about the so-called sexual and racial harassment. Will we male WASPs ever hear the end of these cliché claims? I get tired of hearing Air Force women complain about us chauvinist pigs. They knew the service was a man's world when they entered it."

—E-6, Air Force

"Yes, women are harassed in the military. . . . Nevertheless, both females and males must keep in mind that the armed forces were originally for men and not for women. . . . Therefore both sexes should have a little respect for the other's values."

—HM3 Kathryn Keltz
Pensacola, FL

"My recruiter was honest with me. He told me quite frankly that the Marine Corps was interested in *men.* I persisted and he finally said, 'OK, let's see if you're good enough to be a Marine.' I was and here I am."

E-3 Evelyn A. Schmidt
Cherry Point NC

"I can't believe all these women who bitch and complain that they aren't being treated 'like the guys.' I don't want to be treated like the guys, and I don't want to have to be shot up in battle just to win a medal or a promotion. But I'm doing just as much to help the Army as the ground soldiers and the tank jockeys.

PFC Barbara L. Meyers
Fort Bragg, NC

"It's not true that the military doesn't promote women as fast as they do men. I've moved right up the ladder getting rank as fast as possible. And all the guys in my unit complain that the promotion system favors women!"

—Sgt. Cindy Rodgers
Davis-Monthan AFB, AZ

"Personally, I'm one of those women who would prefer assignment to the combat arms. I'm in great physical shape and few men can keep up with me. So where did the Navy stick me? In an office, typing forms all day!"

PO2 Kimberly Ashford
Great Lakes NAS, MI

"There are some women who won't put up with being sexually harassed, and I am one!"

—E-3, Air Force

"I came in the service believing I would be harassed because I am a woman. I was surprised to learn that I am treated as an equal. So far, I love the Air Force."

—Rhonda Stewart
Homestead AFB, FL

"Not too long ago I came into the Navy with so many hopes and dreams that I couldn't fit them into my seabag. . . . I'm sad to say they have all been shattered."

—Joy Hill Payne, USN
Arlington, VA

"Women in the Navy have it made. They are always complaining about not being equal. Bull! They don't go to sea as much as males. A male spending 20 years in the service will spent at least 50 percent of his time at sea, whereas a female may not go to sea at all. To me, not letting females go to sea on combatant ships is saying it's alright to let the males get blown away, but not the females. Are they so much better than males they can't go in and fight?"

—E-5, Navy

"I have lived in the barracks for the past two years and I see what goes on in the co-ed barracks. Women go into men's rooms daily. Seems to me women are asking for sexual harassment."

—Pvt. Jackson Sloane
Ft. Knox, KY

Before You Sign-Up!

So, you think you might want to join the military? Well, fine. But do you *really know* what awaits you in the military? Is the military profession really what you think it is?

Most young people who join the military, of course, don't truly consider themselves as entering a profession. So they don't inspect too closely before they "buy" into it. To them, it is often a stop-gap measure—a place they can be for 2, 3, 4 years or more while preparing for a more promising future life as a civilian. Very few enter the military with plans of making it a life-long career. As one young woman related, "I'm not interested in the military as a profession. I just want to go in, do my 4 years and learn a skill I can use as a civilian."

Another young recruit told us she joined the service "because I didn't have anything else to do. There aren't many good jobs around for women my age so I'm going to get my act together in the Army for a few years."

A lot of young people join the military service to "get their act together." Some want to see the world. Others join for patriotic reasons and a desire to serve their country. There are many other reasons why a woman might decide on military service.

Unfortunately, many who enlist or accept a commission express surprise when, after only a few weeks or months on active duty, they find service life to be far different than what they had expected it to be.

Having observed thousands of new service entrants—male and female—over the years, we note that it is the rare individual who really knows what she is getting into when she joins the service. After they are in—locked in, to be precise—many a young person has deep regrets about signing on the dotted line down at the recruiter's office.

Can You Trust the Recruiter?

Recruiters tell rosy tales to the interested young person who comes to their office for information and advice. If the recruiter is Marine, then of course anything and everything about the Marine Corps is just superb: job conditions, leadership, facilities, pay and benefits, and everything else. "You won't find it so good in the Air Force, Navy, or Army," he'll say. The problem is, recruiters from the other services will tell you the same thing about *their* respective military branch.

Let's face it: military recruiters are salesmen. Their job is to "sell" their branch of service to the interested prospect. Salespeople do not voluntarily tell a prospect about the disadvantages of their product, now do they? It's not that recruiters lie: as a matter of fact, most are honest and trustworthy, regardless of what you may have read or heard. But honest or not, recruiters are trained, career military personnel. They *believe* in the official version of service life, and recruiters take great pride in praising military virtues. Therefore, it is quite natural that a recruiter emphasize the advantages and play down the negative aspects of his or her branch of service.

Women face a particularly difficult obstacle when they seek out a recruiter and ask him to tell it "like it really is." The truth is it's harder for a woman to enter the service, she has fewer job choices, and once on active duty, she may find things tougher than she expected because of the macho, "male only" attitude of a few men in uniform. But you really should not expect the recruiter to tell a woman applicant all this. Why stir up a hornet's nest? Better to gloss over these facts and, when directly questioned, parrot the official service line—namely, that women are afforded every opportunity available to men. After all, the recruiter may reason, "it's not me that makes the rules. It's the politicians and the brass in Washington, DC."

Regrettably, a large number of the 350,000 people who enlist each year do so with only a minimal amount of accurate and complete information. They are either completely in the dark about what to expect, or else they come in with false expectations that everything will be as the recruiter promised.

How About the Advice of Uncle Bob . . . and Others?

Military recruiters aren't the only ones who provide misleading information about military life. A relative, neighbor, or a friend may likewise fill a person's mind with incorrect information. Uncle Bob may tell his niece that "back when I was in the Army, things were terrible. We lived in substandard barracks, and the food was atrocious." The problem is, Uncle Bob may have been in the Army back in 1955, and a lot of changes have occurred since then. It's almost a whole new ballgame, but Uncle Bob still pictures military life the way it used to be.

On the other hand, a service veteran friend or relative may tell the interested young prospect about how great things used to be. "Pay's great and you can see the world—and afford it," they might say. Here again, old, hearsay information can be misleading. Perhaps the informant was stationed in Germany or Japan before inflation hit in those countries, driving prices higher than in America. Again, such advice and information, while well-intended, can be woefully inadequate.

Anyway, whatever you hear from veterans of military service, remember that conditions for women have dramatically changed in a relatively brief period of time. Uncle Bob and other veterans probably never saw a woman pick up a tool box or even wear grimy work uniforms. In fact, until just a few years ago, it was rare to even see a woman in uniform at all. Of course, today, visit any military base and you'll see plenty of women, and they will be performing every type of job, white and blue collar.

Unrealistic Expectations

Trusting in a recruiter or a veteran can lead to false or unrealistic expectations. This is probably the reason why an incredibly high rate of attrition occurs in the services. Studies show that almost 35 percent of first term military women never make it to the end of their contracted-for term of service. Instead, they are discharged early for disciplinary reasons, failure to adapt to service life, and other reasons.

So how can you avoid unrealistic expectations? Well, reading this book is one way. But up to now, we have mainly discussed the positive features of military service. Sure, we talked about some of the barriers and inequities that exist, but we also pointed out the excellent job opportunities and the many advantages of service life—security, travel, training, and so forth. These advantages exist, and they are the reason why nearly 200,000 women have donned green, tan, and blue uniforms. Still, there are those disadvantages that should be covered.

Private First Class Ruth J. McManus inspects the engine and cooling system on an Army 2½ ton truck (U.S. Army).

The Negatives

If you were to travel to a number of military bases and posts as we have, and talk to active duty servicewomen, you would find that their complaints can generally be categorized in one of eight broad areas:

- Basic/recruit training (boot camp).
- Physical fitness requirements.
- Dress and appearance rules.
- Working hours.
- Lack of privacy.
- Team pressures on individuals.
- Military discipline.
- Officer-enlisted caste system.

In addition to these eight areas of complaint, the authors add an additional negative of military life—the inherent danger of combat.

Now, we caution that what is negative or a minus to one woman may, in fact, be a positive feature of the armed forces to another. Take the matter of basic/recruit training, also called boot camp. Not many people appreciate the rigors of boot camp; but surprisingly, a good number of women laud its benefits. They explain that while in boot camp, they learned a lot about themselves—their capacity, ability to learn and endure, etc.—and they made many lasting friendships. So, what one person may consider a terrible experience another may deem a worthwhile event or set of circumstances. Therefore, as we discuss these potential negatives of service life, you must judge for yourself whether these are minor or major concerns for *you.* You may even decide that one or more are not concerns at all.

The Danger of Combat

We have over 25 years of military service to our credit, and never once have we heard a military woman or man complain about the possibility that, someday, they might be involved in combat. Yet, for every person in uniform, the danger of combat, the possibility of being killed, maimed, or captured, looms large.

In most instances, women in uniform have less to worry about in this regard than do men. It is DOD policy that women be excluded from combat when possible. Note the last two words: *when possible.* The problem is that in a tension filled world, with women assigned to hot spots in the Middle East, in Berlin and West Germany, and other conflict-prone points, the potential for their being involved in combat is great. If, for example, the Russians blitzkrieg across the Fulda Gap into West Germany, our women soldiers and airmen will be on the front lines. Indeed, anywhere in the world, when a U.S. military installation is attacked by aggressive enemy forces, everyone must defend the post—and themselves.

Naturally, most Americans have reservations about killing others, even in wartime. We hold life sacred. But if you take on the responsibilities of becoming a member of our fighting forces, and that's what they are properly called, you may be called upon to fight and to kill. And you accept the risk, however small, of being killed. We say this not to frighten you, but because we want to be honest and straightforward.

It is important you understand that even if you are not involved directly in combat, in time of war or conflict, you may be faced with the results and consequences of war. In her moving and compelling book, *Home Before Morning* (Beaufort Books, 1982), former army nurse Lynda Van Devanter talks about her experience in Vietnam. Lynda says her idealistic view of the war vanished quickly. She worked long and arduous hours in cramped, ill-equipped, understaffed operating rooms. She saw friends die. Almost daily, she witnessed catastrophic injuries to soldiers and civilians. After one traumatic year, she came home, but home turned out to be equally devastating. Working in hospitals brought back chilling scenes of hopelessly wounded soldiers. The war that was fought halfway around the world, and then only indirectly by Lynda, had followed her home.

Lynda Van Devanter's chilling story is not all that unusual. The military needs capable nurses like Lynda, as well as women in most other fields and occupations. These people are classified as support personnel, but the scars and internal damage done by war and battle weigh heavily on support people, too.

Although nurses and other support personnel would not be sent directly into combat except in an emergency crisis, everyone in uniform trains for that eventuality. For example, you will be required to undergo some training, maybe for only a day, on firing and cleaning a military rifle and/or handgun. Also, you may become involved in combat exercises—practice war sessions in which you don gas masks, carry a weapon, man a security post, or otherwise prepare for attack.

An example of this occurs at the Marine Corps base at Quantico, Virginia. There, for a full week, about 40 Navy nurses get the feel of combat. It's a part of their curriculum at the Navy's Health Sciences and Education Training Program. During the week, dressed in combat garb, the nurses sleep in tents and discover the joys of eating C-rations. They talk about amphibious operations, learn of the horrors of nuclear, chemical, and biological warfare, and study how to deal with severe wounds and casualties. Chemical protection gear is worn up to two hours a day. At the shout of "Gas," the nurses have 9 to 10 seconds to put on their gas masks. "That's all the time they would have in a real emergency," says Lieutenant Commander Elizabeth Hart, the program commander.

"It is very important that all health care professionals know how to perform under adverse conditions," comments Rear Admiral Frances T. Shea, Director of the Nurses Corps for the Navy. "As far as the Navy is concerned, the time for women to learn these necessary skills is not during those (combat) conditions, but prior to them."

Admiral Shea's comments are realistic and professional. As a military woman, you must be prepared for the eventuality of combat. Unless the United States becomes embroiled in a major war or a conflict like Vietnam or Korea, the likelihood is small you'll be putting your life on the line or suffering through the trauma that nurse Lynda Van Devanter experienced. But if the whistles do blow, and war is imminent, don't count completely on women being spared.

At an army training post where women trainees were learning how to fire the M-16 rifle at the firing range, one young woman decided she didn't want to pick up her weapon. Reluctantly, she looked over at the sergeant in charge of the firing range and said, "I didn't join the Army to go out and kill anyone. I have never fired a gun and don't want to now."

"Naw," he replied sarcastically, "you didn't join the army at all. You thought you were joining some social circle. Well, I got news for you, Private. Pick up that weapon!" The young woman sighed, picked up her weapon and began the firing session. Her scores were surprisingly high.

Boot Camp

Everyone dreads it, but it's the initiation fee you will have to pay if you decide the military is for you. The movie and television show, *Private Benjamin*, exemplifies the utter shock and surprise that can befall an unsuspecting new recruit as she arrives at boot camp.

In the movie, Private Benjamin, humorously portrayed by Goldie Hawn, protests to her drill sergeant at boot camp that she "didn't know it was going to be like this. How about the condominiums and the fancy restaurants my recruiter told me about?" she asks. Unfortunately, Private Benjamin found that boot camp was mostly getting up at the crack of dawn, endlessly drilling and marching, spit-shining combat boots, and cleaning up toilets. And the condomimiums? Sorry, Private Benjamin, the only thing the Army had available was crude, open bay barracks with communal facilities.

Actually, boot camp—more accurately recruit or basic training—isn't all *that* bad. The first few weeks are tough but things get easier as time goes on. You will live and work with 50 to 80 other women who will soon know more about you than you do yourself. You will be faced with rigorous physical conditioning programs. And you will also be tested for what you learn in academic classes.

Oh yes, you will march, and march, and march, until your feet feel as if they aren't part of your body anymore. But before too long, marching will become second nature with you. You'll even find that you really *don't* have two left feet, as your training instructor claims. You'll also notice that as time goes by, you are more capable of passing those terribly picky locker and room inspections. Since you finally learned how to dress by the regulation, the dress inspections, in formation, become a breeze.

Until you do learn the ropes and start doing things the way your training inspector demands, boot camp won't be fun at all. Perhaps the worst part is the criticism that you and every other new recruit receives. Americans don't take to criticisms very well, but at boot camp, superiors will carp on everything, sometimes just to see how well you stand up. Some criticisms will be just; others won't. Instead, they will be designed to test your durability and perseverence under stress.

Specialist 4th Class Kimberly Stafford, parachute rigger with the U.S. Army Garrison Presidio of San Francisco, packs one of the parachutes which will be used by Airborne Reserve units on the West Coast (U.S. Army).

For example, you'll be "picked on" for a small thread on your shirt's button hole, for a fingerprint on your shiny belt buckle, for a bit of dust on your shoes, or because your hair is 1/16 inch longer than regulation. Your instructor will tell you your bed looks lousy, your footlocker arrangement is "the worst she's ever seen" and that you march like a gorilla. Take heart. She probably won't be singling you out. It's just the normal treatment everyone gets in basic training. Still, if being criticized like this for admittedly nitpicky and "Mickey Mouse" infractions disturbs you to the point you can't function mentally, you could have a problem.

Naturally, no-one likes "Mickey Mouse" games or to be treated like infants—as many recruits claim they are treated in basic training. The thing to keep in mind is that it's *not forever.* In a few weeks, through your perseverence you will have proven to your instructor you have what it takes to be a member of the service team. Things will then lighten up. There are some individuals who cannot take even a day of such brusque and seemingly unfair criticism. If you are one of them, don't sign on the dotted line down at the recruiter's office.

However, we hope that fear of boot camp won't deter you from enlisting. Have faith when we tell you that time will fly and that after boot camp is over, you will be proud of your accomplishment. You will be a bonafide member of the best military force in the world.

Physical Fitness Requirements

Physical fitness for the military woman doesn't end with graduation from boot camp. It continues throughout your time in service. The level of fitness you are expected to maintain varies with the type of job you have. For example, it is obvious that perons in the direct combat skills—paratroopers, combat controllers, Green Berets, etc.—are required to stay in peak physical condition. However, as a support person, you will not be held to these same high standards.

It should be pointed out that group physical training, such as that required of paratroopers and other combat units, is the exception rather than the rule. Watching old war movies and television shows often leads people to think that service life is highly regimented; that, for example, everyone works out every day as a group in full fatigue uniform. However, in real life, only a few military units are physically oriented. The vast majority of service people are *encouraged* to keep fit and they are provided time during the duty schedule for a physical fitness regime. For instance, one supervisor may allow the people who work for her an extra hour off each day, in addition to an hour for lunch, to jog, play racquetball or tennis, or participate in another physical activity of the individual's choice. Another supervisor may give her people an entire afternoon off each week.

The services make it easy for their personnel by providing the equipment and facilities necessary for athletic activity. Every post of any size has a well-equipped gymnasium, with a steam or sauna bath, weights, basketball and racquetball courts and a variety of athletic equipment and supplies (from boxing gloves to baseball bats) an individual can check out and borrow at no cost. Also, most military installations provide excellent jogging trails and paths, swimming pools, tennis courts, baseball and football fields, and tracks.

Participation in organized group activities is also encouraged. Almost every military installation has a comprehensive intramural sports program where one unit plays another unit in friendly competition. Typical sports in the intramural program include softball, baseball, basketball, and touch football. Also, some military installations have traveling post or base-wide sports teams that compete against other base teams.

Is Weight a Problem For You?

While we are discussing physical fitness, we should talk also about the problem of being overweight. There is a maximum allowable weight that each service allows its members to reach. Members who exceed this maximum are placed in a formal weight reduction program. The individual is given a reasonable period of time to lose the undesirable number of pounds. If she cannot, she is honorably discharged.

Is this maximum allowable weight set very high so that really only a monstrously obese person would be in jeopardy of being forced out of service? No, indeed. In fact, one study published in a service publication found that two-thirds of all the members of professional football teams would be classified as *overweight* by the military! Even the heavyweight boxing champion of the world was found to be "too fat" to enter the service. This study certainly disproved the allegation by some that the services' standards were too lax.

If you are now overweight according to service standards, you will not be permitted to go on active duty until you have shed the excess weight. You can plead that you are physically fit—even that you are a world-class champion in weightlifting or wrestling, but your pleas will fall on deaf ears. Each service has a weight chart it uses. These charts generally use two criteria: height and weight. The taller you are, the more your allowable weight. You also may be interested to know that each service has a *different* standard. In other words, you may be overweight as far as the Army is concerned, but meet the standards of the Air Force or Navy. So, if you have been rejected as being overweight according to the service that is otherwise your first choice, you conceivably could seek out one of the other services and find you qualify. However, it would seem a shame for you to not, first, attempt instead to take off the excess pounds by a safe program of diet and exercise.

The weight standards for each branch of service are outlined in Figure 6-1. These were the standards as this book went to press. However, these criteria are subject to change, so use them only as approximates. Phone or see your recruiter for current standards.

Weight Standards for Women
(Maximum Allowable Weight)

Height (In Inches)	Weight: Army	Air Force	Navy & Marines
58	113	126	121
59	117	128	123
60	121	130	125
61	125	132	127
62	130	134	130
63	134	136	134
64	138	139	138
65	142	144	142
66	147	148	147
67	151	152	151
68	156	156	156
69	160	161	160
70	165	165	165
71	170	169	170
72	175	174	175

Figure 6-1

Dress and Appearance Rules

One of the things that servicewomen — and men — complain about most is the military service's insistence that the individual uniform conform to the dress and appearance rules established by each branch of service. Each of the five services has a regulation that prescribes *exactly* the uniform to be worn and how it is to be worn. That regulation also explains the acceptable hairstyles. Furthermore, it tells you the shoes to be worn with each uniform — even the color and type of any umbrella carried while in uniform.

Women used to selecting their own clothing, as most women are, and wearing it in their own style may find frustrating the military system of prescribing, by regulation, the manner in which they are to dress and appear in public.

A few women object to wearing the same uniform day in and day out. They bemoan the lack of variety. Still others complain about the color of their uniform. They say that green (the typical army uniform) doesn't look good on them, say, or that blue (the air force uniform) doesn't match their hazel eyes. Indeed, quite a few women openly admit that they chose a particular branch of service because they preferred that service's color or style of uniform.

It would seem frivolous to sign up to spend several years of one's life in one or the other of the services merely because the uniform is "neat" or of a preferred color. On the other hand, who wants to wear green (or black or whatever) day in and day out if he or she loathes the color? Actually, few people would admit that the color or style of a particular service's uniform motivated them to enter *that* service. Probably such a factor is just *one more* reason why someone would finally decide on a specific branch.

Objections to the Uniform

Some people object to military service not because of the color or styling of a specific uniform, but because they object to the wearing of a uniform at all. These people claim that to have to conform to what someone else mandates concerning what to wear each working day is degrading and takes away from a person's individuality. "I don't want to be an automaton—I want to be a real person, with the ability to wear any wardrobe that suits me," one recruit remarked.

Is this a legitimate concern? Perhaps. But not everyone thinks so. Some people are even relieved that, after joining the service, they no longer have to concern themselves with the difficult task each day of deciding what they will wear. As one airman explained, "When I used to work for an insurance company, every day I had to figure out which set of clothing I would wear—would *this* belt go with *this* skirt and this color with that, and so on. Now? Ha! It's the same uniform every day. Sure saves a lot of time and worry."

Many people do not mind wearing the uniform because they consider it a symbol of our nation and what the nation stands for. They take pride in wearing the uniform and in looking as sharp as possible when in uniform.

It is probably a bit much to claim that being required to wear a prescribed set of clothing stifles one's creativity or individuality. As one Marine told us, "It's what's in your head that counts, *not* what's on your back!" In any event, one should keep in mind that it is *not only* the military that requires a certain dress code of its employees. Nor are uniforms worn only by military people.

In a recent Air Force personnel newsletter, an Air Force sergeant commented on the requirement to wear a uniform. She stated that many civilians believe a uniform makes the military person a cog in a faceless mass. Yet, the sergeant noted, uniforms are common in civilian occupations and few wearers protest.

The sergeant went on to illustrate her point by relating an incident that occurred when she stopped for dinner at a nationally known chain restaurant. While there, she struck up a conversation with several waitresses and attendants who noticed that she was wearing a military uniform.

Why, asked one waitress, would she want to enlist in a uniformed military service where everyone looked alike. "Yeah," chimed in another restaurant employee, "I value my individuality too much to be told what to wear and all."

The sergeant stated that these comments appeared rather odd, considering the fact that both of the employees wore cute little hats and red dresses. She also noted that the cooks at the restaurant all dressed in black trousers and red shirts—all which had the chain's name on their collars and cuffs. Oddly enough, all the employees wore name tags.

"Don't you mind wearing the same dresses, hats, shirts, and trousers the 50,000 other employees of this chain are wearing all over the country," she inquired.

"Why," the surprised employee responded, "it never crossed my mind."

The Air Force sergeant discovered the fascinating truth that one's attitude does color the perception of whether something, such as required clothing, is an undue restriction. Wearing the uniform and obeying military regulations about appearance can be either an onerous, despised requirement, or a condition of service which is gladly and willingly accepted. It all depends on your own perception. Karen, for example, each day wears the white uniform of the nurse, yet she doesn't mind at all. She's proud to be a nurse and proud to be an armed forces officer, and her white uniform is symbolic of the pride she feels inside.

So, it's up to you. You can expect the military service to tell you how long your hair can be, which buttons must stay buttoned on your uniform blouse, and what type of jewelry is acceptable to be worn with your uniform. You can be directed to keep your shoes shiny and polished and your skirt cut to a certain length. It's all part of the military lifestyle. But there's one thing to keep in mind. Except in time of war or during special periods when a war exercise is being conducted, as a member of the armed forces you will work about 8 hours a day, just the same as most civilian workers. After normal duty hours, as work time is called in the military, your time is your own. That means you can wear any civilian clothes you like, set your hair just the way you want to, and be your own person in regard to appearance.

Work Hours

Speaking of "normal" duty hours, you might be interested in knowing just what working hours are for military personnel. We mentioned that most likely in the armed forces you would work eight hours a day, the same as civilians. You can also expect to put in an average of 40 hours per week. However, this is not always the case; sometimes military people work very long hours—much more than 40 hours per week. Not all military jobs can be accomplished on a Monday through Friday schedule, either. Keep in mind that the security of our nation depends on the women and men of our armed forces being vigilent and ready. This vigilance and readiness must be constant: 24 hours a day, seven days a week and 52 weeks a year. The question is, how does this affect you as a member of the armed forces?

Well, first, it means that regardless of your job or career field, you might be required to work on the weekend or perform shift work in the evening or late at night. It also means that you may have to work on a holiday. This can be a tough thing to do when you realize that, while you're working, others may be enjoying the holiday. On important family occasions, such as during Easter and Christmas, this can be a particularly irritating situation.

Work Schedules Vary

Generally, during holidays and even on weekends, military commanders attempt to give their people as much time off as possible. So usually this is not a problem, but sometimes it is. For those who work in jobs such as security or military police, fire protection, and aircraft, safety and rescue, working during periods and times when the normal workforce is off is a way of life. This is true of personnel in units and with jobs that require them to be on alert.

For example, there must be at least a number of pilots on air force bases and naval aircraft carriers ready to hop in their planes and taxi down the runway when the whistle goes off. Crews also are on call deep beneath the earth in missile silos available to perform duties in event of strategic attack by the enemy.

It might be well to keep in mind that Pearl Harbor occurred early on a Sunday morning. American military authorities are dedicated to making sure that never again is our country to be caught unawares, by sneak or surprise attack. For the average soldier, airman or seaman, this need to be ever ready and watchful means a work life and schedule that, in civilian life, would be considered unacceptable.

Usually, if you have a job in one of these fields, you won't have to work *every* weekend or *every* holiday. The supervisors try to spread the bad times around so everyone has his share and no more. But you can expect your name to be on the worklist at least on occasion.

However, it is not merely the folks in the jobs with 24 hour a day missions who work odd hours and during weekends and holidays. Inevitably, there will be periods when *everyone* must join in. For instance, every military unit practices combat exercises in which all personnel are told to leave what they're doing at home and come to their workcenter *immediately.* Sometimes, a telephone call comes early in the morning when you are fast asleep. At other times, maybe you are in the middle of a fantastic TV show with your feet on a stool, kicking back with a drink, joined by nearby friends. Sorry, pal, drop everything and rush down to the office or staging area, the military site where alerted people congregate and await instructions. And report in full uniform, sometimes with a full duffel bag.

On such occasions, who knows whether this alert will be the real thing or just another practice exercise. If it's for real, you may be required to board a ship, airplane, bus, truck, or other vehicle and be gone for an undeterminate period of time. Your destination? Who knows. What of your family, if you have one locally? Well, they'll just have to fend for themselves. That's part of military life.

The military feels it has first priority in your life. Therefore, your time is, in the military view, their time. And don't expect to get paid time and a half for overtime. Your salary is always the same while you're in the armed forces, no matter how many hours you toil. Naturally, your supervisors have a responsibility to be fair and to not require you to work more than 40 hours a week unless absolutely necessary. Just remember that all military supervisors are rated on how well they manage their subordinates. If they abuse their subordinates by forcing them to work long hours unnecessarily, they can be held accountable. Still, if the military mission needs to get done and it means putting in overtime, you, as an individual, do not have the option of saying, "sorry, I have personal things I have to take care of." The services just don't work that way.

Lack of Privacy

Everyone knows that service members are often called GIs. But did you know what the "GI" stands for? It means *government issue.* Thus, the venerable term GI implies that even people, individual service women and men, are owned body and soul by the government. Obviously, this is an exaggeration of the true situation. Yet, there are elements of fact to the assertion that the government—the military—"owns" its people. This shows up most in the area of personal privacy.

It is common to hear military women complain of a lack of privacy. There are many realms of your life that are subject to scrutiny while you are in uniform. For example, your commander may obtain access to your past performance record, to your medical records, and even to your personal history. If you will be handling classified documents or working with classified equipment, you may be subjected to security checks by government investigators. The service will claim it has "a right to know" all about you, and it might. Nevertheless, it is a little unsettling to realize how transparent life can be in the armed forces. One's privacy can even be breached each day after work because military authorities also control where you live and, to some extent, *how* you live.

Living Arrangements

Probably the biggest complaint of single people in the military is living quarters. Often people beef that they have little or no privacy and that, compared to the married serviceman, a single person is treated unfairly. Many claim outright discrimination against singles. Let's look at some of the more commonly heard grievances of inequity and allegations of invasion of privacy.

Single service people, male and female, *can be required* to live on base. As a matter of fact, most enlisted, single people do reside on the military installation at which they are assigned. Commanders often allow them to live off the installation but refuse to pay single people a housing allowance. Married people of all ranks, however, *do* receive this housing allowance. As a result, singles find it difficult to afford an apartment or home off the installation unless they accept roommates.

The living quarters—barracks, dormitory rooms or apartments—of single people living on a military installation can be inspected at any time for "health and welfare" reasons, which means whenever and for whatever reason the commanding officer sees fit. Periodically, the commander may have drug sniffing dogs, accompanied by military police, go through the on-post living quarters. If during such an inspection the authorities find drugs or anything else of an illegal nature, it will avail you little to holler that your Constitutional rights against search and seizure have been violated. You've "bought the farm" and you'd best get yourself a good lawyer.

Many of the buildings reserved for singles' living quarters afford little privacy. Officers have things the best. Senior officers have their own apartments; two junior officers share an apartment. For many enlisted people conditions are bleak. Career NCO's usually are assigned individual rooms with a refrigerator and a divan. Lower ranking enlisteds only dream of such privacy. The Army still has many open-bay barracks. These are the ones with one huge room in which as many as twenty people live. No walls. Little privacy.

It doesn't take much imagination to think about the problems such a lack of privacy creates. For one thing, occupants of these barracks frequently complain about the volume of their fellow residents' stereos. Most of these barracks have a common dayroom where the service has provided a television for the entire population's viewing pleasure. Who decides which channel to watch?

The trend in all the services has been toward individual rooms (two or three per room), an ideal the Air Force has had for many years. The Navy, for space reasons (not much room on some ships and in submarines), often doesn't meet this ideal nor does the Army in many cases. Even in the Air Force, most enlisted dormitories have communal bathrooms. Many enlisted people complain bitterly of this lack of physical privacy. Combined with the services' use of health and welfare inspections of on-base living quarters, this lack of privacy may result in the single person calling it quits after her first tour in the service is completed.

Interestingly, married service people living on base in military family quarters are left alone; their residences are considered inviolate and sacrosanct. A commander may complain if their lawn is not mowed or if their dog roams loose, but the *inside* of the home is theirs. The old American saying, "A man's home is his castle" applies to married service members, *but* not to singles.

However, there is at least one instance when all military persons, enlisted and officer, married or single, are not afforded privacy. That instance involves the illegal use of drugs, including marijuana. While the military law enforcement authorities do not always exercise it, courts have held that the military's jurisdiction is complete in the case of drug abuse. This means that a pot party in a civilian residence off the military installation can be the target of a military police raid. Recently, several military persons were court-martialed after it was proved they consumed illegal drugs at such a party. One officer was court-martialed and dismissed from the service for merely attending a party at which drugs were in evidence.

Of course, it is understandable why the military seeks to keep its members drug free and is therefore so strict in enforcing drug laws. It is essential that military personnel be in complete control of their senses and faculties at all times. Another's life may depend on it. It's also important to recognize that many military personnel are entrusted with the safety and care of millions of dollars worth of equipment—from tanks, to computers, to hi-tech aircraft and missiles. This is no place for a person high on drugs—or alcohol either, for that matter.

If you are suspected of taking illegal drugs or abusing alcohol, if you are arrested for drug possession or an offense such as driving while drunk, you can be required to attend mandatory counseling as well as be subject to punishment by court-martial or other means. Repeat offenses may result in a discharge, or imprisonment for major infractions. The armed forces don't consider this invading your privacy. Instead, they feel it's a matter of protecting property and personnel.

Other Privacy Considerations

There are other facets of an individual's life that the military monitors or becomes involved with in a manner that some feel conflicts with the basic right of privacy. For example, personal automobiles are subject to search while on a military installation as is the physical person of individuals.

In foreign countries, servicemembers must first obtain permission of their commanding officer before they can marry a foreign citizen. Violators of this requirement are rarely punished, but could be if their superiors decided to enforce the rule.

Military superiors cannot sell anything of value to subordinates (supposedly even a used auto).

Servicemembers can be discharged or have a "black mark" inserted in their official records for failure to pay just debts. Civilian firms may report your delinquency to your military superior who may then "strong arm" you to pay the debt.

Servicemembers are prohibited from actively engaging in partisan political activities other than voting. You can't, for instance, be a delegate to the Republican or Democratic Party Convention.

Members of the military services cannot participate in a political demonstration while in uniform nor make speeches unauthorized in advance by military authorities.

Any traffic offenses or minor law violations of military personnel can result in some form of administrative sanction or punishment by a military superior. This is in addition to any penalties given or assessed the individual by civilian authorities.

Any and all bad checks written on base are reported to an individual's immediate commander and supervisor.

While overseas, military personnel are responsible for the behavior of their families. If you are in the Army and your teenage son mugs a lady, *your* military performance report could suffer. If your husband gets a traffic ticket, *you* are called in by your commanding officer to explain why.

Officers are forbidden from many social associations with enlisted personnel, as will be explained in the next chapter.

All military personnel are subject to being required to provide a urine or blood sample to determine whether or not they have been using illegal drugs.

Military commanders can restrict individuals to the confines of the base, not permitting them to even visit off-base. Usually this is done only in times of emergency or unusual conditions.

Fair or Unfair?

Some individuals feel that the privacy one sacrifices outweighs the benefits and advantages accrued from military service. They point out that military personnel are held to higher standards and have fewer civil rights than do civilians. However, others disagree, holding that the sacrifices in privacy are necessary evils required to insure the security of military bases, boost the image of the military in the civilian community, and insure that the armed forces are disciplined and ready for combat. Where you stand on this matter may well determine if military life is for you.

Team Pressures on an Individual

Sometimes its hard to be an individual in the military. For one thing, there's that huge bureaucracy to contend with and a lot of red tape to be found. However, it is important to realize that it takes people—teams of people—to accomplish the military mission. After you join the service, you may occasionally feel that you aren't your own person, that you are being forced to conform to group pressures and do what the "team"—the other members of your service unit—want you to do, regardless of your individual desires. When this feeling hits, keep in mind the importance of a team effort.

In any career field or job in our society, those who have a knack for getting along with people seem to receive the bulk of promotions and career advancement. The fact is that practically all important advances and accomplishments of modern society are achieved only by an intense *collective* effort. For instance, the day of the long inventor, like Alexander Graham Bell or Thomas Edison, working way into the night to create innovative new machines or procedures, is for the most part over. Today, large corporations and scientific laboratories employ teams of scientists, designers, engineers and inventors to work on specific new inventions or improvements to existing products. Rarely does a person work alone on a project.

A Chief Petty Officer assists Equipment Operator Constructionman Camella J. Jones of Gold Beach, Oregon, as she learns how to operate a large crane. She is the first woman of the Navy to qualify as a heavy equipment operator and to be assigned to the U.S. Navy Construction Batallion (Naval Photographic Center).

Often, this teamwork aspect of military service is compared to a football or basketball team. For instance, while one or two players on a football team may be extremely talented, it is doubtful they could be successful without the entire team working together in an organized fashion. One cannot imagine a situation, for example, in which the fullback decides he wants to run to the left with the ball even though the quarterback calls for a sweep to the right. In basketball, even a superstar must be passed the ball by her teammates and receive blocks and screens to assist her in making shots. This sports analogy is equally applicable to military goal accomplishment.

It is also important to realize that in the military, like the sports world, you may not necessarily like all the team players. There might be that obnoxious gal from Iowa or the wiseguy from New York. You may be required to work with people who do not share your taste in music, food, and entertainment or your opinions on morality or lifestyle. Nevertheless, you will be expected to tolerate their faults (as long as they tolerate *yours*, of course) and to treat them as part of the team. Remember, in the service it is the *military mission* that takes precedence and not the personality, quirks or personal desires of the individual.

The military highly values a person who can get along with others, who can be just as good a follower as she can be a leader, and who can put the group's success ahead of her own desires and goals. Private industry—in fact, just about every arena of American society—also holds such a person in high regard.

Many intellectuals and other extremely bright and talented individuals lack this important quality of cooperation and team spirit. Some people refuse to mesh their efforts with others because they are afraid they will not be the leader of the group. Others resent peer pressures placed on them by group members.

On the other hand, many women enjoy working with others in a cooperative manner. They enjoy the camaraderie and friendships that develop. If this is your temperament, you will find the service to your liking.

Comments from Military Women and Men

"I wish someone in the know had taken me aside before I joined the Marines. I mean, boot camp is tough, but I never figured it would be *this* tough!"

—Marine Recruit
Parris Island, NC

"The military pay recently has vastly improved. And the thing is, when a recession hits, no one talks about laying off soldiers. I'm not saying everything is great in the Army—there's a lot of B.S. But, it beats a soup line."

—Sgt. Mary A. Ford
Ft. Benning, GA

"My recruiter told me the entire truth—that boot camp was hard and that I would be pushed physically. Too bad I didn't listen close enough. Man! I wish I was home!"

—E-1 Army
Basic Trainee, Ft. Polk, LA

"Boot camp is really easy. I had harder times in the Boy Scouts. I didn't like losing most of my hair, though. I look and feel like a member of a punk rock group."

—AB Gordon Randall
Lackland AFB, TX

"I was stationed in Korea right on the demilitarized zone, and I actually saw what war was."

—Sp 4, Vernard Feggus
Hg. Co
Fort Riley, KS

"The very nature of a military environment and the demands that it can impress on all members should be enough to provide the incentive for them to maintain a high level of physical fitness."

—CW4 Jeanette Sears
Ft. Sill, OK

"The Air Force is losing more military managers than ever before. I'm forced to live in a barracks, use a meal card, and pull details like shoveling snow . . . and I am a career sergeant! I wish the Air Force would treat me like a manager in civilian life."

—E-5, Air Force
Chanute AFB, IL

"We in the Navy have it a heck of a lot worse than does the Air Force. On board ship, E-1's through E-9's sleep in racks with no privacy and very little locker space. E-1's through E-3's have to have liberty passes to leave the ship."

—OS2 Randall Leash
USS Alamo

"Even though, after four years service, I'm looked up to as a supervisor at work, within the barracks nothing has changed. I still have to share a small room, clean up the community john and put up with constant inspections and harassment because some people aren't clean or neat. Civilian single people aren't treated like this."

—E-4, Air Force
Edwards AFB, CA

"I got this to say about complainers . . . if you can't handle the load, get off the road. Remember, no one promised you a condo."

—YN2 Brian Gott
USS Ajax

"When I first saw my basic training platoon sergeant, I thought to myself, 'there's a pushover.' That's where I made my first mistake. I stuck my hands into my pockets and he yelled, 'Private, get your hands out of your pockets . . . ' Right away, I knew the ballgame was over."

—Pvt. Leonard Lusher
Fort Eustis, VA

"When do I get a chance to get some sleep time? It's go, go, go, go in Officer Training School. I'm about 'gone'."

—Air Force Officer Trainee
Lackland AFB, TX

"Mickey Mouse is still alive and well! She's here at Fort Polk. She's my training instructor and she performs her nitpicky act every morning by prancing in my barracks and finding a million things wrong. So what if I forgot to make my bed? Mickey Mouse says, 'tsk, tsk!' "

—E-1, Army
Basic Trainee, Ft. Polk, LA

"One day, here on campus, I encountered an Army recruiter armed with dozens of pamphlets. I didn't pay much attention until she started talking about the many benefits and opportunities available to me. Sounded good. Still, do I really want to be in Army green?"

—Roberta L. Brandt
Army ROTC Cadet
University of Tennessee

"At 5:10 a.m. the bugles blared and we darted out of our room for formation and PT (physical training). After roll call, we jogged to the field for warm-ups and the mile and half run . . . at the chow hall there were plenty of demerits if you weren't careful—eyes straight ahead, no talking, feet flat on the floor when eating. Oftentimes we had only four to five minutes to gobble down a meal . . . I felt good about myself and what I could accomplish."

—Anne McRae
AFROTC Cadet
Villanova University

Military Discipline and the Officer-Enlisted System

The young enlisted women had exited her dormitory and walked only fifty feet or so when, from behind, she heard a bellowing voice, "Soldier, don't you salute commissioned officers?"

"Yes," protested the woman as she turned to face an officer she had just passed on the sidewalk. "But I didn't notice you."

"Didn't notice me? Well, in the future keep your eyes open!"

"Okay," replied the soldier.

"Okay?" the officer interjected abruptly. "Didn't you learn in basic training to address officers as Sir? By the way, stand at attention when I talk to you."

"Yes, Sir," said the frightened young airman, quickly coming to a brace.

True story? Yes, indeed. Scenes like this do occur in the military services. And they illustrate one important fact: whether the Air Force, Army, Navy, Coast Guard or Marines, there is a vital difference between two social classes of persons—officer and enlisted. In fact, it would be more accurate to say that there exists in the armed forces a great chasm between these two groups.

Rank Has Its Privileges

The unequal relationship between military officers and enlisteds is a strange anomaly in our democratic American society. It would be easy to say that officers are the upper class and relegate enlisteds to the lower class. But this division would not be fully descriptive of the unique class structure found in the military services.

Many enlisted women believe the officer-enlisted system to be unfair and undemocratic. They point out that officers are treated almost like royalty or bluebloods, with exclusive "perks" or privileges granted this "class" of personnel. On the other hand, they contend, enlisted people, who make up the bulk of the military's personnel, are treated as an inferior class, devoid of privileges.

What privileges are they talking about? Well, there are many advantages to being an officer. One, of course, is higher pay and fringe benefits than that received by enlisteds. But the military services have instituted a social system that affects the everyday lives of service people much more than does money alone. This system is called RHIP—Rank Has It's Privileges.

The old military saying, "Rank Has It's Privileges," means exactly that. The more rank one has in the military, the more positive benefits one accrues, socially and while on duty. When an outside observer views the difference in rank and status given officers versus that of enlisteds, it is easy to see who in the services gets the lion's share of privileges.

The superior privileges implied by RHIP and granted the officer may seem minor and even peculiar to civilians; but within the military, they constitute a respected and hallowed ritual of rights *due* officers *by* enlisted persons. The requirement to pay homage to officers is a sore point for many enlisted personnel, some of whom feel it is demeaning and detracts from their own dignity as fellow human beings. As an enlisted Marine once related to us, "Officers expect you to grovel in front of them."

What's the Difference?

If you're not sure of the difference between an officer and an enlisted person, let us clear away the cobwebs. Officers are the management class in the armed forces—the higher leaders. Almost all are college graduates, some have master's degrees; a few possess doctorate-level degrees. Officers achieve their status by passing an officer's candidate test and by completing an officer training course. This training course might be the college ROTC program, an in-service officer training or officer training school, or attendance at one of the service academies; for example, the Air Force Academy in Colorado or the U.S. Military Academy at West Point.

Enlisted personnel are usually high school graduates though some have the high school GED test equivalent, and a few men are accepted without a high school diploma or its equivalent at all. Enlisted persons generally enter by passing with minimally acceptable scores the service entrance exam (ASVAB), then attend and complete basic training, or boot camp.

The lowest ranking officer is a second lieutenant, the highest a four-star general. In the navy, these ranks are called ensign and admiral, respectively. For enlisted persons, each service has its own title for the lowest rank—private in the army, airman basic in the air force, and so on. Each service also has its own peculiar name for those in the highest enlisted rank; for example, the Army's top ranked person is addressed as sergeant major; the Navy's as master chief petty officer; the Marine's as either sergeant major or master gunnery sergeant.

Each branch of service has a rigid seniority system for promotion; consequently, it takes many, many years for an individual to rise to the top ranks. Indeed, only the sharpest and most deserving persons achieve the highest ranks.

Within each category, officer and enlisted, are supervisory levels. Most enlisted personnel are not supervisors, but a great number are, and they exercise considerable authority. However—and this is important—the lowest ranking officer has more authority and exercises more authority than the highest-ranked enlisted person. This is true regardless of how smart the enlisted person is and also true even if the enlisted man or woman is better educated, older, has more seniority or whatever. The military is a hierarchy, and the officers sit at the pinnacle of the hierarchical pyramid.

Officer Privileges

Because the military is a hierarchical organization, power flows from the top down. The higher a person is in the hierarchy, the more privileges she/he will have, and the more the people lower on the totem pole will have to demonstrate their recognition of the person's superiority. The services are set up to reinforce this concept of RHIP and, day in and day out, everyone is reminded of his or her own place in the overall pecking order.

Among the privileges of rank accorded officers are the following:

The Place of Honor: When a person junior in rank walks, rides, or sits with a person of higher rank, he takes a position to the left of the senior. Also, the junior person should allow the senior to be the first to enter a door and the first to take a seat in a meeting room or office. The ranking person also departs the room or office first.

Attention: The physical position of "attention," as those of you who have seen a movie or television show with a military theme well know, is one where the body is erect and braced. Eyes stare zombie-like and straight ahead; arms hand stiffly at one's sides. Feet are together with toes pointed out at a 45° angle. When a high ranking officer enters an area in which there are juniors, this is the position required, at least until the superior officer gives the command "at ease."

The Salute: Enlisted persons are required to render a crisp hand salute when meeting an officer outdoors and in some cases indoors. This requirement, the services contend, is not intended to represent subservience by the enlisted person to the particular officer being saluted (Capt. Smith, Lt. Jones or whomever). Instead, the services state that the act of saluting recognizes the respect the enlisted person *must* pay the officer *because of his or her status as an officer.* In other words, according to the services, the salute is a show of respect to the office and not the person holding it.

Forms of Address: The terms "Sir" and "Ma'am" are mandatory for military conversation. It goes without saying that if you prefer "Yeah" or even a plain "Yes" to "Yes Sir!" service life for you will prove difficult, if not untenable. While Sir or Ma'am are always safe terms when addressing a superior officer, enlisteds also may use the officer's rank (Colonel, Lieutenant, etc.) as a title. "Good Morning, Bob" will get you in a world of trouble if you are enlisted and Bob happens to be an officer.

Behavior: It is very important that enlisteds not direct anger at an officer, nor should they use any language which might be construed as an insult or ridicule. Military law calls this type of behavior either *insubordination* or *disrespect* (take your pick). Both are punishable by stiff penalties. Even an untoward (or misinterpreted) facial gesture could get you in trouble!

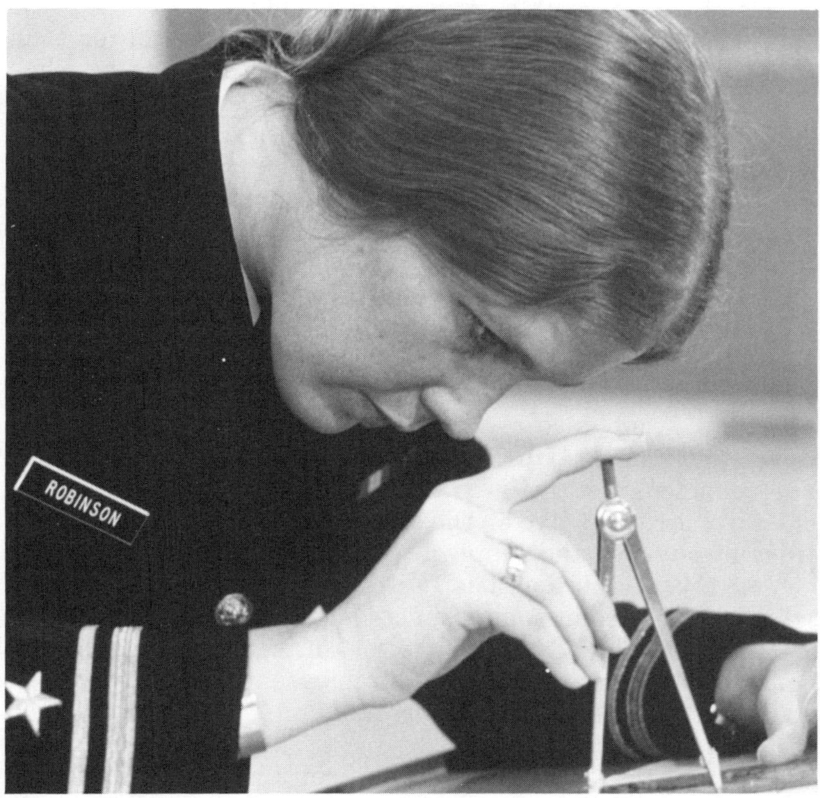

Lt. j.g. Sherry Robinson is the first woman naval officer to attend Air Traffic Control School at the Naval Air Technical Training Center (Naval Photographic Center).

Civilian Comparisons

All the privileges of rank outlined are required because of the services' rigid adherence to the concept of military rank. The services claim that such privileges are benign. Courtesies such as saluting, addressing superiors as "Sir," and allowing a senior to enter and depart first, say the services, are mere signs of respect. And, they claim, similar requirements for courteous behavior can be found in civilian occupations.

In this view, deference by juniors to a senior official or manager is by no means an onerous requirement. It is pointed out, for example, that managers and supervisors in civilian industry are also addressed formally. It is unlikely, for instance, that an assembly line worker would fail to call the president of General Motors by any form of address other than "Mister" or "Sir." Likewise, courtesies such as standing when a civilian superior enters the office are customary.

However, the military services are more rigid in one sense. Failure to use the proper form of address or to extend a courtesy can result in lawful punishment under military justice statutes. In civilian society, you might lose your job if you refuse to address your superior as "Sir." In the military community, you can be sent to jail!

It is difficult for civilians who never spent time in the service to comprehend the gap that exists between the officer and the enlisted. Some sociologists equate this distinction to a caste system, such as that found in India or in other less developed nations. Obviously, this is an extreme view when one considers the pitiful status accorded the "untouchable" class in India, who live on the streets under intolerable conditions of poverty and hunger.

Yet, there is in operation in the military a social system which resembles in some aspects a caste-based society. It is a system in which the two groups, officer and enlisted, are considered separate, unique, and in essence, segregated. As an officer once told us, "Officers and enlisted men are like oil and water—they don't mix."

The military's social system is firmly rooted in historical experience and it is reinforced in practice through the military's legal and social networks.

Historical Roots

The existence of two separate groups in the military, officer and enlisted, has its roots deep in military history and traditions. The United States military was certainly not the first to draw the line between the officers and enlisted. Such great military generals and tacticians as Hannibal, Caesar, and Alexander the Great made a distinction between the elite commander or leader of men and the common soldiers over whom he was in charge. In past centuries, when the Kings of France, England, Spain, and the Italian and German principalities ordered their forces into battle, the royalty led the way. The gap between the leader and his men was often great. "Officers" in these ancient and historical military forces were not to associate with the common horde; for instance, they had their meals alone or with trusted aides who were also officers. They also had such privileges as servants, arms bearers, and better shelter. Even their fighting equipment (swords, lances, shields, uniforms and horses) was of higher quality.

The fledgling military forces of General George Washington, during the Revolutionary War of the 1770's, also made a distinction between officer and enlisted. Men of property and education were granted officer status while others—laborers, tenant farmers, and other "common folk"—were relegated to enlisted status. The social division between the two classes of soldiers was great. For example, just prior to the famed Battle of Valley Forge, in which Washington and his men crossed the icy Delaware River to surprise and rout the British, many enlisted men were heard to grumble and openly complain of their harsh conditions. The bitter cold winter and their lack of shelter and warm clothes did little to soothe their anger and resentment. Some talk of mutiny and possible rebellion was heard among the enlisted men.

Washington, being advised of the talk of rebellion, and aware of the dissension among the enlisted ranks, cautioned his officers to watch closely the activities and behavior of the men under them. "Enlisted men are sly and cunning," warned our future first President, "and not to be trusted."

Legal Distinctions

America has come a long way since the days of George Washington, but the gap today between the officer and enlisted is still wide. This gap is not only a customary one, derived from historical roots, but is, in addition, firmly based in law. The Uniform Code of Military Justice, a set of laws passed by the U.S. Congress, sharply distinguishes between officers and enlisted. Service regulations codify this legal distinction and provide for different rules of behavior on the part of each of the two personnel groups. An officer, for example, is required to meet far higher standards of conduct than is an enlisted person.

In practice, this distinction often means that officers receive stiffer punishments for misconduct than do enlisted personnel—for the same and similar offenses! If, for instance, an enlisted man is arrested for drunk and disorderly conduct, he may get by with as little as a reprimand or perhaps, a small fine. However, an officer arrested for the same offense can expect much harsher penalties, at least a huge fine *and* a reprimand. Often, a minor crime like this will result in the end of an officer's career.

This requirement for the officer to maintain higher standards of conduct than the enlisted person is legalized in many forms. For example, enlisted persons who "keep their nose clean" and don't cause disciplinary problems are rewarded for their exemplary behavior every three years with a Good Conduct Medal. A medal for mere "good conduct!" Officers, however, are not eligible for this medal as their behavior, as a matter of course, is expected to be above board and certainly better than just "good."

Another example of the legal distinction is the services' laws requiring strict obedience by enlisted personnel to the orders of officers. Stiff sentences in prison can result from willful disobedience. In 1975, for example, an Air Force Technical Sergeant, a veteran of 17 years, was convicted by a court martial for refusing to obey an officer's order to shave his sideburns. For his "crime" he was sentenced to a Bad Conduct Discharge and 10 years confinement at hard labor. The sergeant had refused to shave off one-quarter more inches from his sideburns.

Other offenses against lawful authority also are punishable under military law. An airman in West Germany was fined for failure to salute her commanding officer. A seaman on the USS Norton Sound was sentenced to six months in federal prison for "disrespect" to a superior officer. A soldier at Fort Bragg was given a Dishonorable Discharge and confinement for "insubordination."

The services contend that obedience to orders, as well as the show of respect due superiors, contributes to good morale, order, and discipline—elements essential to combat effectiveness. In fairness to the services, these guidelines apply to all military personnel, officer and enlisted. Still, the heaviest burden seems to fall on enlisted personnel.

A distinction should be made, however, between a lawful and an *unlawful* order. No one in the military, regardless of his rank, can order a person to do something that is illegal or unlawful. For instance, a soldier cannot be ordered to shoot an unarmed and unresisting civilian. Nor can a person be ordered to perform a task that is personally degrading or discriminatory or be of personal benefit to the superior. For example, an officer could not order an enlisted woman to undress and perform a sex act, or to call another person by a racial epithet. Also, one cannot be ordered to wash the officers' auto or deliver his personal mail. The order must have a military purpose.

And if You Disagree With the Order?

Generally, a soldier, airman, sailor or marine will be *requested* to perform a duty or task. "Orders" are usually given only if a person doesn't do as "requested." The successful servicewoman not only follows orders, but does so cheerfully. If she disagrees with the order, she may *politely* and diplomatically explain to her superior *why* she disagrees (unless, of course, bullets are flying or bombs are falling, in which case conversation may be somewhat inhibited). However, if the superior insists and the order is legal, she will have to obey.

Social Distinctions

An interesting facet of the distinction between the officer and enlisteds is that the gap between these groups exists even after work or duty hours.

The military has a special term it uses to define the unauthorized social mingling of officers and enlisted personnel: *fraternization.* Regulations state that fraternization between these groups will not be tolerated. Officers who fraternize (that is, socialize) with enlisted troops subject themselves to punishment under the codes of military law.

This is not to imply that all social contacts are impermissible. For example, a unit party or affair in which all members of the unit, enlisted and officer, participate is allowable. The point, of course, is that at unit social events, a military structure, however subtle, still remains.

The rule against fraternization is difficult to enforce because it restricts what many servicemen feel is their personal actions and behavior while out of uniform. As one enlisted man told me, "What I do after work—who I see, and run around with—is my own business!"

The services see things differently. The official view is that familiarity breeds contempt, that officers who socialize with enlisted subordinates sacrifice their "command presence." Not only that, but the *Air Officers Guide* even contends that enlisteds "do not desire or need the social companionship of officers." Service officials say that social mixing after duty hours cannot fail to impact on what happens in the office, shop, or field of battle. In any case, it is not true that any service member has what civilians call "free time." Officially, service members remain on call and available for duty 24 hours a day, 7 days a week.

Service Views

Official service views and philosophies regarding officer-enlisted relations vary, although all prohibit extensive fraternization and equal work status.

The Air Force view is best described in Air Force Regulation 30-1, which states that: "Two important characteristics of the officer and enlisted relationship are loyalty and mutual respect . . . we are all professionals and as such we must treat each other with dignity and respect."

These words are fairly representative of the current Air Force philosophy on this subject. According to the Air Force, close personal friendships are also okay; "However," the Air Force regulation goes on to state, "friendships must not interfere with judgment or duty performance." As far as relations on the job are concerned, the Air Force prohibits officers from "associating with enlisted personnel on a basis of military equality."

Some liberalization can be detected in ever-evolving Air Force philosophy on this subject, but other services are not so modern in view. In contrast with the view of the Air Force is the more strict guidelines laid down by the Army. For example, the current *Guide to Army Social Life* put out by the Fort Benning, Georgia, Infantry School, states that: "It is improper for an officer to get familiar or personal with an enlisted . . . This custom is not snobbery . . . familiarity does breed contempt . . ."

Likewise, the Marines find it hard to accept the liberalizing trend. A recent recruiting pamphlet entitled, *As an Officer of Marines*, had this to say about the subject: "The relationship between officers and men should in no sense be that of superior and inferior nor that of master and servant, but rather that of teacher and scholar. In fact, it should partake of the nature of the relationship between father and son to the extent that officers . . . are responsible for the physical, mental and moral welfare as well as the discipline and military training of the young men under their command."

It is interesting to note that the Marines take a highly paternalistic view of the officer-enlisted relationship. Note also that the terms "men" and "young men" are used rather than more neutral, non-sexist words. Many enlisted people in the military today reject the Marine paternalism as degrading. "I want a leader and a coach," said one young enlisted woman interviewed, "not a father . . . I already have a father back in Albany, New York!"

Segregated Facilities

One sore point of many enlisted people is that facilities of the military community are organized and set up to reinforce the segregation of officers and enlisteds. For example, on most military installations there are separate clubs, dining facilities and housing areas for each group. There are even separate swimming pools on many military bases and posts. In fact, a little over a decade ago, in some buildings on military installations the toilet facilities were segregated!

Some say that this situation of separate facilities smacks of patent discrimination and even a negative form of segregation. Critics point out that the Civil Rights Act of 1963 freed the Blacks and other minorities but not enlisted persons.

However, in fairness to the military, one can find a similar parallel in civilian life. The residential areas lived in by higher paid managers of civilian factories and plants are, after all, not the same as those lived in by the average wage earner or laborer. The country clubs of civilian life discriminate on the basis of economic means and social status just as do the military officer clubs. And not every civilian worker can afford to dine in the better restaurants frequented by the affluent and wealthy. Still, in terms of their impact on military life, separate facilities do solidify the existing distinction between the officer and the enlisted groups.

The Military Woman's Spouse: Officer or Enlisted?

The services categorize the spouse (civilian husband or wife) in the same way they do the member. The wife of an officer, for example, takes on the social aura and many of the same privileges as does her uniformed husband, and the civilian husband of an enlisted woman is himself stigmatized as "enlisted." Thus, the civilian spouse of an enlisted woman cannot join or attend functions at the Officers' club, nor can he swim in the Officers' pool. And, of course, he must live with his wife in the segregated enlisted housing area. The principle that officers should not fraternize with enlisted extends even to spouses.

A New Trend Toward Equality

There has been a noticeable trend in recent years toward equality between the two classes of military personnel: officer and enlisted. In fact, in some work units the traditional view that "never the twain shall meet" has already given way to a newer concept that calls for a relationship more closely approximating the typical civilian manager-worker environment.

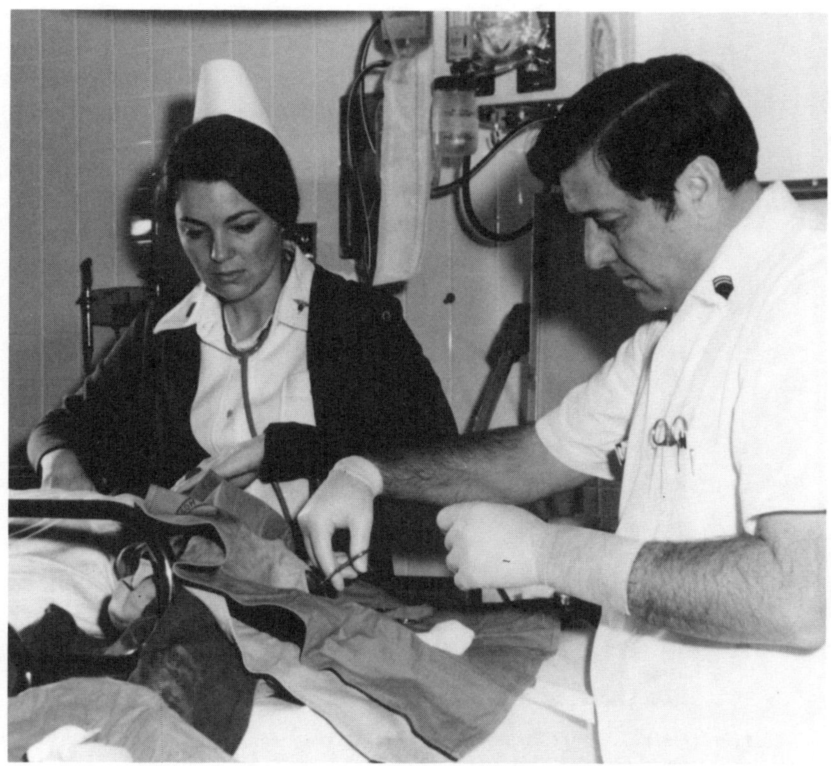

First Lieutenant Catherine Siby assists Hospital Corpsman, SP6 Phillip Bolino in suturing a wound at Kimsbrough Army Hospital, Ft. Meade, Maryland (U.S. Army).

The thawing of relations seems to be more pronounced in the Air Force, a branch of service traditionalists accuse of being "just a bunch of civilians in uniform." However, the movement toward more equality has also taken hold to some extent in the other services, especially in those military units in which the enlisted personnel possess a high degree of skills and education.

Today, in military units such as engineering and computers there is not much difference in the education backgrounds of the officer and enlisted persons. This fact inhibits a superior attitude or behavior on the part of the officers.

In some of these units, a friendly environment of equality exists to such an extent that officers and enlisteds are on a first name basis. The services frown on this type of familiari-

Major General Mary Clarke, the highest ranking woman in the U.S. Army and commander of Ft. McClellan, Alabama, chats with Specialist Four Joanne Loomis prior to the first all-female parachute jump at Ft. Bragg, North Carolina (U.S. Army).

ty, but in the privacy and safety of the individuals' shop and work section, it is a practice which is becoming more and more common.

However, in the combat skills areas and wherever else one finds a disparity between the educational level of the officer and the enlisted person, the rigid separation of the two groups continues. Thus, there has, in fact, arisen two militaries: (a) the traditional, hardcore military in which strict observance is demanded to the officer-enlisted division, and (2) a more flexible military in which enlisted personnel are on a much more equal footing.

The Mellowing of the Fraternization Rule

Many of the social barriers implied by the term fraternization are today falling by the wayside. The growing numbers of women entering military service over the last decade has heightened the demise of these barriers. It is becoming more and more common to see male and female service members, of whatever rank of status, dating and even marrying. It is one thing to tell a male officer he can't go bowling, dancing or out to dinner with enlisted male friends. It is yet another to tell the same officer he must refrain from these activities with an enlisted member of the opposite sex.

The fact that many officers and enlisteds have in recent years openly disobeyed the regulations prohibiting fraternization has caused a mellowing of the rules. Thus today, while these regulations still exist, superior officers often look the other way when a junior grade officer *occasionally* socializes with enlisted persons. However, a *pattern* of fraternization by an individual officer can result in disciplinary punishment. As a minimum, the officer's career will be hurt.

You and the Officer-Enlisted System

You may be asking yourself just what all this means to you as you ponder whether or not to enter military service. We believe that you should not be overly concerned with this issue. While the military system of officer-enlisted categories and strict obedience to superiors is far different than the typical civilian work environment, there are rules set up to guard against abuse. Also, it is a fact that the enlisted woman who tries her best to contribute to the mission of the service and works hard in doing her assigned job will be treated with the respect and admiration that her efforts deserve.

The scene depicted by the idea of the snobbish officer lording it over those he deems inferior, the enlisted forces, is not truly accurate in today's military. The vast majority of military officers are not power-hungry elitists who go around using their rank and authority to make life difficult for enlisted people. Quite the contrary, most are decent men and women sensitive to the needs and feelings of their subordinate personnel. Generally, those who aren't good managers of people usually are found out early in their careers and they are either separated from the service, or made to mend their ways.

Comments from Military Women and Men

"My CO (Commanding Officer) is all-Marine. And that's why I like him. He's an officer but he's a Marine!"

—Cpl. Robert Riley
MCAS Beaufort, SC

"Lieutenants need to have enlisted people show them how to tie their shoes. It's disgusting when you realize they are supposed to be better than you."

—Airman
Bergstrom AFB, TX

"Officers have their place and enlisted people have theirs. Personally, I don't care to associate with officers because they aren't *real* people."

—Sr. Airman
Offut AFB, NB

"Enlisted swine? Why, they're okay, but I wouldn't want my sister to marry one! Just kidding, of course."

—Army Captain
Ft. Polk, LA

"Who cares what rank a person is? The question is, do they know their job and do they do it?"

—1 Sgt. Karina Tomlin
Ft. Bragg, NC

"Officers are just people, like me. *But,* I don't think I should have to 'sir' them and salute all the time. I'm sick and tired of being a second-class citizen."

—Jackson R. Timball
Great Lakes, NAS, MI

"Right before I reached my one-year mark I was a hopeless case . . . My chiefs and division officer helped me by caring and listening to my side of things. Now . . . I love it (the Navy)."

—E-3, Navy

"My first gripe is that nobody listens to the airmen and lower NCOs. Oh, sure, the Air Force has its Chief Master Sergeant of the Air Force, who goes around with his bulging wallet and placates the 'working class.' And there's the IG, and the congressman, and all the other people who are making megabucks to help the 'little guy.' But do they listen? Do they care? My answer, as a long-time observer, would be an emphatic NO!"

—E-6
Air Force

"Yeah, the pay is pretty good, but look at what you have to do to get it. I don't like officers and NCOs acting like they're God and I'm a peon cause I'm an E-2 soldier. And as far as the base exchange, I think Sears and K-Mart have better prices."

—Pvt. Sloane T. Davis
Ft. Lewis, WA

"Although I am an E-9 and feel that I earned those privileges that come with rank, I do not believe in letting that rank go to my head. My rank does not give me the right to take advantage of others. I earn the respect of others by my actions, not my rank."

—E-9, Air Force
Melbourne, FL

"I am married and live off-base. I can barely afford it because Marine Corps housing is for E-4 and above. I personally think that this is totally unfair. E-4s and above make more money than I do, and they can afford to live off-base. I pay $275 a month, plus utilities. I feel that this rule is an act of discrimination against low-ranking Marines. I also feel that we should have the first chance at the cheaper base housing."

—E-3, Marine

Special Concerns of Women

Women *are* special . . . would you agree? One day while shopping, we ran across a couple of interesting posters. One blatantly stated, "Behind Every Successful Man is a Hard-working Woman." The second one depicted a worn-out secretary, laying across her desk of piled-high paperwork. It stated, "They Found Someone to do the Work of Five Men—One Woman." Sayings such as these bring a smile to our face. But maybe we can learn from these strong, but subtle outcries from frustrated women. Women are hardworking, reliable, dedicated, capable members of our society.

Since before our lifetime, women's role began evolving and will continue to do so for centuries to come. In the past, women have been nurtured and coddled as the weaker sex, never really being able to prove their true capabilities. One friend told her father of her aspirations to become a doctor. Her father was surprised and voiced his concern. He stated, "But you are a girl; you are supposed to get married and raise children. You should be a nurse, marry someone, and then you can work part-time if you want. It is always easy for a nurse to find a job."

This man is an extremely dedicated father, but his ideals were a product of the era. Such were the ideas of the time only a few years ago. Now young girls are taught they can do anything a boy can do. Even selecting a military career has become more acceptable.

The Equal Rights Amendment proposal has opened the doors for many women to seek positions that were unfulfilled dreams in the past. Now that women have moved into the workforce in mass, they are entering the military services in great numbers also. With increased numbers of women now in our armed service, some very special concerns need to be addressed.

Pregnancy

We thought we would address this topic first since it does set women apart from men. After all, no one could argue that this is not a special concern for women. The pregnancy of women is a matter of great complexity for the armed forces, and it is an issue that has caused much dissension between the two sexes.

You cannot be pregnant when you enter active duty in any branch of the military. If you are, and do not tell your recruiter, you will probably find yourself being discharged from the service once it is discovered. It would fall into the category of a medical condition existing prior to entering active duty.

The military no longer discharges women when they become pregnant, as it used to do. Today it is an option. If you become pregnant and decide to leave the military you must see your commanding officer, and he will decide if you are to be discharged. If your career field is in short supply, or if you have just completed an expensive training program, your request for discharge may well be denied.

While on active duty, the military completely pays for your medical expenses. If the military installation where you are stationed does not have obstetrical services, you may find yourself being transported to a nearby hospital where you can deliver your baby. Some bases have contracts with town or city hospitals where you can receive complete obstetrical care at government expense.

Okay, you know the care is available, now what do you do if you are pregnant? First you need to visit your base medical facility. Even if your base does not have a hospital *per se*, the laboratory services available are usually capable of performing urine pregnancy tests. If by some chance, you are at a remote area without such facilities, your supervisor can guide you to such services. If your test is positive, you need to schedule an appointment with a physician or other health care provider. As an active duty member your work environment will be investigated by the base Environmental Services. This is to determine if there are any potentially hazardous characteristics to your work that may harm you or your baby.

A letter will be forwarded to your supervisor explaining your condition and your expected delivery date. You must also obtain a doctor's medical statement which outlines the restrictions during your pregnancy. Every branch of the military requires such a report. Basically it will state how many pounds of weight you are allowed to lift, how many hours a week you can work, and what physical activity you can perform. This is designed to protect you and your unborn child.

From now on you will establish an obstetrical medical record. You can expect expert medical care throughout your neonatal and post-partum period. Morning sickness is so very common with pregnant women. This is a normal, though uncomfortable, symptom of pregnancy. Most of the time you will be expected to perform your duties throughout this period. If you are unable to do so, medical care is available.

Maternity uniforms are obtainable in all branches of the military services. You will need to see your supervisor and supply officer for procurement of them. Pregnancy may limit you or deter you from certain work tasks; nevertheless you will be expected to perform your duties as long as you can—up to the last moment. If light duty is called for, you will be assigned light duty.

Maternity leave ranges from 4 to 6 weeks depending on your branch of service. If medical problems exist, extensions may be authorized. Most branches of the service expect you to be within your weight limit within three months after your child is born.

Many male co-workers frown upon women who become pregnant. They feel they do not carry their workload. Pregnancy is a natural condition; in the majority of cases you should be able to be an equal carrier of the workload. Still, you will be absent from your duty shop or office during the delivery and recovery period. And men may point out that *they* are required to take up the work slack in your absence. They are correct. Your pregnancy means more work for them. This is one of those thorny issues that has not been satisfactorily resolved and maybe never can be.

The Single Parent

It is not unusual in this day and age for women to take on the great responsibility of raising a child alone. At this time the military no longer accepts single-parent women unless they designate a guardian for their child. Guardianship requires legal documentation presented to your recruiter. Once this is completed you may be considered for entry to the military service.

If you get married before or after you enter active duty, you can then apply through legal channels for your child to become your legal dependent, along with your spouse if applicable.

You may wonder why the military discriminates against single mothers. Well, it is only recently so. With the divorce rate being so high, single mothers were seeking military careers in an unbelievable number. This led to severe problems such as child care. Congress no longer felt that we could adequately meet our country's defense needs, so single mothers were no longer accepted unless child-guardian criteria was met.

Child Care

It tragically happened at an Air Force base last year. The General was worried and more than a little upset as he drove past the base parking lot and saw the many children sitting alone in cars, temporarily abandoned by their mothers. Their moms were airmen assigned to combat-ready Air Force units at the strategic base commanded by the General. Some of the mothers were single, others were married to servicemen. Awakened in the early hours of the morning, these military women rushed to the base and began preparing to embark on an air mission to an undisclosed location. There was, however, one major problem: what to do with the kids?

Luckily this was an exercise, the seventh for the year, and the mothers were soon reunited with their kids. But if it had been the real thing, the mothers would have had only a short time—perhaps as little as 15 minutes or less—to find someone to take care of their children during the mother's absence. The base General realized this was an impossibility. He knew that the military women who had left these kids in parked cars might soon be unexpectedly up and flying halfway around the world, for who knows how long. As a result of incidents like this, all the military services have issued stern warnings to military mothers.

As a responsible parent, single or married, you must provide adequate child care for your child. Not all bases have a base child care center at your disposal. If they do, they may be overcrowded. Either way it will be up to you to provide adequate child care. This will be an additional financial requirement. You also must designate a non-military guardian for your child. This person must be available at a moment's notice, in case you are called upon to perform your duties elsewhere in the United States or overseas, or a war breaks out.

Airman first Class Jane B. Hoapili, a ballistic missile analyst technician with the 381st Strategic Missile Wing, McConnell AFB, Kansas, (U.S. Air Force).

You may be presented with military orders to an assignment where dependents are not allowed—a remote tour. This means there is no housing or medical care available to dependents. Again, you will have to call upon your child's guardian to care for your child. This may be weeks, months or years. Even if your spouse is military, you may have different assignments, whereby neither of you are able to care for your child.

What happens if your child becomes ill? Can your military supervisor spare you to care for your sick child? Not necessarily. What if you were the only mechanic scheduled to be on duty and an aircraft has an emergency failure? If you are a military nurse, who will relieve you and care for all your patients? You may also be required to use your vacation time during the illness of your child.

Child care is one of the biggest problems faced by military parents. Child care should be considered before you decide to have a child. But if you do decide to be a mother, remember that your military service will not make special allowances for you to care for you child. It's *your* responsibility.

Officer-Enlisted Romancing

We briefly discussed officer-enlisted social relationships in the preceding chapter. According to our armed forces, *fraternization* between officer and enlisted personnel is prohibited. This means there is not courtship or romancing, for example, between a male officer and a female enlisted woman. Now both you and we know, as long as we are on earth, social relationships between men and women will develop. This is of course what mother nature considers normal. But as long as the military has been in existence, it has frowned upon male-female, officer-enlisted relationships. What, you may ask, is all the concern about?

The traditional military view is that good order and discipline requires immediate, loyal, cheerful compliance with the lawful orders of the superior. Experience and nature show that these cannot be readily attained when there is undue familiarity between the officer and those under his or her command.

It is very difficult for the military even today to distinguish fraternization from an acceptable relationship between two people with common interests. With societal changes and the increase of women in the military, relationships naturally do commonly develop between females and males. Well, can you be disciplined for this relationship? Yes, possibly. With the world's present move for equality, is the freedom of the individual to choose his or her own companions being curbed? Actually, yes.

The traditionalist who wishes to separate officers and enlisteds contends such relationships are harmful. He asks, can an officer woo an airman one night and admonish the same person the next morning?

There are many obstacles to hurdle on this subject. Should the traditional view of no fraternization be adopted and those participants be disciplined? Or a more modern view with the fear of decreased operational effectiveness?

Presently, it is best to respect your superior, develop a sound working relationship, and shy away from "office" romances or even romancing with a supervisor outside your immediate organization. Men and women have actually been court-martialed for socially dating or having sexual relations with persons of the opposite sex whom they outrank. Some claim this is undemocratic, but it is the reality today, and if you wish to become a member of the armed forces, it undoubtedly is best to understand the reality of military service.

Gays Prohibited

While we are talking about relationships in the services, especially between officer and enlisted persons, we should devote a few words to the issue of gay, or lesbian, relationships.

The services' policies prohibit lesbians and homosexuals from entering the military. If, once on active duty, a person is found to be engaged in a homosexual or lesbian act, that person is swiftly discharged from the armed forces. The military believes that the gay person detracts from morale and good discipline. Whether or not you agree, if you believe yourself to be lesbian we strongly recommend that you do not enter the armed forces. In the first place, you would have to lie to the recruiter who will definitely ask you if you are lesbian. In the second place, you would have to continually hide your sexual preference once you were in uniform.

The prohibitions against romances between officers and enlisteds apply to any kind of relationship, whether heterosexual or homosexual. There have been cases in the armed forces in which lesbian and homosexual relationships have been discovered. Invariably, those persons involved were quickly separated from the armed forces. There have also been instances of sexual harassment in which a military superior who was a lesbian or homosexual exerted pressure on a lower ranking individual to submit to sex. Such cases are rare, but when they do occur and are documented the services act swiftly to punish the offender.

Sexual Harassment

We discussed sexual harassment in an earlier chapter but the subject is important enough to cover a few more points.

What is sexual harassment? It could be a few pats on your behind consistently, or maybe your boss likes to call you sweetie or honey. It could be as blatant as a request for sexual encounters in order for your career to progress. Does this exist in the military? Unfortunately it does, but you have rights and can do something about it.

All too often women do not report these activities because it involves their male peers or superiors. Who are you hurting more? Are you going to continue being treated like a sex object? You do have supportive services available to you.

A young woman nurse went through a terrible ordeal. She worked in a large medical center. Her supervisor was a colonel. He consistently used suggestive language and attempted to get her alone. Her work was finally suffering because she tried to avoid him at all cost. She really didn't understand the system and feared if she reported him, her career would be jeopardized. She suffered two years until she was reassigned. No one should have to tolerate such acts as they are strictly forbidden by every service.

In the armed forces, these cases are taken very seriously. If you are unfortunate enough to find yourself a victim of sexual harassment there are several avenues you can pursue. You may report it directly to your supervisor. If your superior does not cooperate or is the person in question, you may take your case to the next higher superior. All officers and enlisted persons have a commanding officer or similar overseer of the welfare. The complaint may also be reported to an Equal Opportunity counselor who is required to completely investigate the situation as presented.

According to service rules, sexual harassment, as with any other form of arbitrary discrimination, is intolerable. Official policy is that people who engage in such practices violate professional standards, insult human dignity, and also diminish mission effectiveness.

In the military services, hundreds of complaints are investigated, and many lead to the ruining of careers. As a result, sexual harassment is becoming rare because it is a sure and quick way to jeopardize one's military career. As long as men and women work and live together there will be suggestive remarks and sexual pressures. This is not the military's problem alone. Even in the civilian world this exists. But at least in the armed forces, there are avenues of assistance to pursue.

If you perform your job or duties well you will gain the respect of your male peers and will tend to be accepted for your capabilities and not your sexual gender or feminine characteristics. But in those rare instances when a military supervisor or superior breaks the rules and attempts to sexually harass you, remember: You don't have to accept this crude and unbecoming treatment. Don't suffer . . . do something about it.

Separation From Family and Husband

Everyone likes to see a happy family living harmoniously together and no one enjoys separating a loving couple. The military is no different. However, because of its huge mission to protect our country, home and families, sacrifices sometimes have to be made. For example, not every assignment you encounter will allow your husband and family to join you. Many times it is due to the job characteristics or the remote sites or distant countries where your military base is located.

Being away from your family is not easy but the time can be used to your advantage. You could take a college course or learn new skills and enhance your work performance. Military members pitch in and support each other when their families are away from them. So you never really are alone. There are many support systems for your distant family to rely on. They have full use of all military facilities in their area. They can use the medical facilities, PX (Post Exchange or department store), commissary (grocery store), base theater, hobby shop, and the list goes on.

What if you find yourself married to another military member? What are your chances for being assigned to the same base? Well, if you are both in the same service, it helps; but the military's job requirements come first. Of course, all the services are concerned with preserving the family unit. But what if your husband is stationed on a combat vessel? Perhaps you can be assigned to his port base. Sometime one of you may have to decline a career-broadening assignment for one less appealing to you, so as to maintain a common household. What about the children if you are separated? Who will they stay with? If your husband is civilian, how will he feel about leaving his job to follow you? These are all very common situations.

With the increased number of women entering the military services, marriages to another service member are more common than ever. The military is not always able to assign the husband and wife to the same installation. For example, the husband may be a pilot and the wife an accounting officer. If he is reassigned to a base where pilots but not accounting officers are needed, she is stuck. The military may be unable to find a specific base where *both* a pilot and an accounting officer are needed at the same time. No matter how hard they try, you may find yourself separated from your family.

One Navy woman related her particular situation to us. She and her Navy husband spent the first year of their marriage living 2,000 miles apart. Reunited for two years, the Navy then separated them again for almost two additional years. So in five years, they were apart almost four. This type of situation can promote both financial and emotional strains on a family. Sometimes one of the military members has to give up his/her career even though it is promising.

You need to be aware of the rising dilemma that faces the military. To preserve the family unit while maintaining operational readiness can be difficult.

Moving With Your Family

It is a big expense to move your family and your household goods around the country or overseas. For most military people, the armed forces foot the bill. However, for enlisted personnel with less than two years of military service, the cost is theirs alone. After the two year period, the government pays to move your belongings. But think of the opportunity you and your family have. You can see parts of your own country and visit foreign countries that most people only dream about. Your children would have a marvelous education in store for them. They could visit, learn, explore, and live the cultures of many countries. The experiences received may be worth the expense and sometimes the inconvenience of moving.

Of course, once you get to where you're going, you will need a home, apartment, or other housing for you and your family. Some women who enlist say they were told by their recruiter that free housing would be made available to them on the base or military installation to which they are assigned. Actually, base housing for families is limited and not always available. It is your responsibility to find suitable living quarters for your family. Many times, due to limited housing availability in foreign countries, this could be an added expense. Indeed, you may even encounter problems finding adequate housing at some stateside locales. As your career progresses, base housing is more available. You will many times have the opportunity to live among the people of foreign countries—a very rewarding, if not somewhat unique experience. You may not always live in the best housing at first, but things do get better.

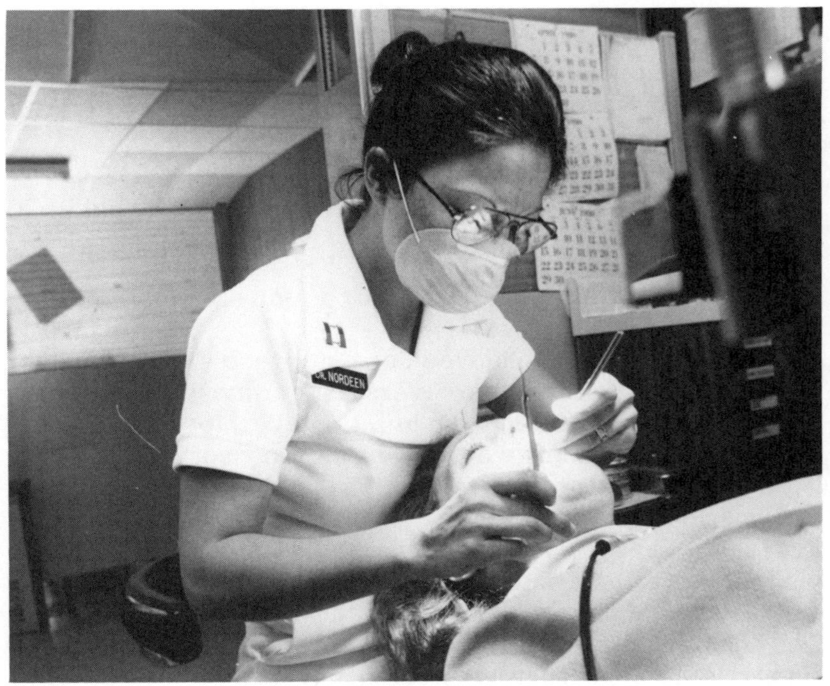

Captain Jeannine Nordeen (Dr.), Army Dentist, is making a gold crown for a patient.

Health Care

Health care is one of the greatest concerns to all of us. In the military services the military member and her dependents (husband and children) receive medical care at the expense of the federal government. Outpatient clinic care is completely free of charge. Inpatient care (hospitalization) requires a nominal fee of a few dollars a day for dependents.

Many military posts have medical hospitals, complete with pediatrics, obstetrics and gynecology clinics. Others have fair-sized clinics to handle routine care. If service isn't available at the base, military people are referred to local civilian doctors and facilities and the government picks up the tab. In such cases, the government will pay most, but not all, the costs of civilian medical service for dependents.

Dental care is provided for all active duty service members, but generally not for dependents. Some overseas bases or specific dental programs do offer dependent care on a limited basis. When possible, emergency care is authorized.

Comments from Military Women and Men

"I live off the base. I am a single woman without dependents. I have the same bills as married people. Because I haven't had children, does this mean I deserve less pay? When you signed that contract, it was under equal terms."

—E-4, Air Force
George AFB, CA

"We added up all the advantages . . . the choice was clear—we re-enlisted. Such benefits as an excellent retirement plan, complete medical care, and outstanding educational opportunities are things you can't find in other careers."

—Sgts. Ted and Carla Bednarski
McCord AFB, WA

"Like it or not, females are here to stay. I served on board a Navy vessel for two years and it was no joy ride. I was in and out of port; away from my husband for months at a time. I don't want sympathy. I just want to show you that females are doing the same as you are, and more. Do you return home from work every day to a baby, laundry and all the other joys of home? I'm not complaining. I love it! At least I know I can handle it, what about you?"

—E-4, Navy

"I think that just the experience of being in a foreign country is outstanding. In all the small towns we were in during a recent exercise, (the Germans) would bring us food, coffee, and gifts. We would exchange unit crests, airborne wings—whatever we had to swap."

—2 Lt. Joseph Herrera
A Company, 1st Infantry Division

"I am fed up hearing about the supposedly great benefits that we military members who are married to another military member receive. We do not get any special consideration because we both work for Uncle. We do our share of TDYs, remote tours, and PCS's, sometimes leaving the base, but for different locations at the same time. We have to sign a form agreeing to leave our kids in the custody of others in case of a military emergency, TDY or overseas base evacuation."

—E-5, Air Force
Anchorage, AK

"I have been in the Navy for three years. I'm seriously thinking of making a career out of it, except for one thing. I am a bisexual male. Our society of gays within the military would like one question answered: Why is the military so against us? We pose no threat to our nation's security, we are Americans, we are proud to serve our country. Yet, we are treated as common criminals when caught. We are court-martialed or discharged."

—E-4, Navy

"The military does things for a reason. Most enlisted people who date officers have shown they don't want to follow that officer's orders because they feel, 'I'm dating this officer. Why should I do what he or she tells me to do?' I am a corporal in the Marine Corps and my wife is an officer in the Army. When we are in uniform, even just outside our house, I treat her as an officer and a lady."

—E-4, Marine
USS Guam

"I would like to say a few words on the matter of sexual harassment. Yes, women are harassed in the military and civilian areas, but so are many young and older men. Therefore, both sexes should have a little bit of respect for the other's values."

—HM3 Kathryn Keltz
NAMI, Class 82-1
Pensacola, FL 32508

Profiles of Success—How Women Can Get Ahead

On her desk is a plaque that reads, "Women Have to Be Twice as Good." Rear Admiral Pauline Hartington is living proof that the woman who truly desires to succeed in the military can do so.

Hartington is the top woman operational officer in the U.S. Navy. If you enlist in the Navy, you may run into her. She's the head of the Naval Training Center in Orlando, Florida, a boot camp center for both women and men.

Admiral Hartington didn't get where she is overnight. Achieving the rank of admiral is tough for anyone, especially a woman. But like other successful military women, she set out to prove to an unbelieving world that women can not only function but excel in the armed forces.

As many women already on active duty will tell you, it's not always easy being a woman in uniform—not in a male-dominated military society. Still, thousands of women are at this very moment holding challenging jobs and proving their value to their branch of service. This chapter will describe the contributions of many such women.

If you are considering military service, but wonder if it's truly the place for a woman, these vignettes of women in uniform should provide assurance. There's the example of Major General Norma Brown, the able commander of the Air Force's Chanute Military Training Center, and Navy Captain Grace Hopper who, at the incredible, ripe old age of 77, is regarded as one of the world's foremost computer experts. Both General Brown and Captain Hopper have reached the top ranks of the military profession and their grand accomplishments show just what a younger woman with ambition, drive, and dedication can achieve.

There are other success stories here, too, that should inspire a woman about to begin her "journey" in our nation's armed forces. For example, the story of Marilyn Henry, once an auto mechanic and now an Army chaplain; Ensign Brenda Robinson, the first black woman to be a Navy pilot; and Air Force Lieutenant Judith Urey, who has the authority to ground an entire fleet of planes.

For excitement and drama, we have included the fascinating stories of Airman Bonnie Richardson, one of only 54 women in the armed forces who works as an explosives disposal specialist; and Army PFC Cynthia Beard who specializes in jumping out of aircraft.

All of the women described in this chapter are living their lives fully and richly. They've shaken off any stereotype of women as the weaker sex—as persons who can't "make the grade" in the military. Their example, as well as that of thousands of other women not discussed here, is important. It illustrates what you yourself can do once in uniform. So, once you've enlisted or accepted that commission, step right out and prove yourself. Wherever you are stationed, in whatever job you're assigned, just remember the examples and heed the advice of the women who have gone before you.

The Air Force's Top Woman Training Commander

Even at first glance, the Chanute (Illinois) Technical Training Center looks more like a college campus than a military installation. Mature ash and maple trees line its streets and shade the red brick classroom buildings that seem to bob up unexpectedly in the huge sea of lawns meandering through the facility.

This was the first impression of USAF Chief Master Sergeant Dave Sheeder as he visited Chanute to research his article, *A New Way Of Life*, which appeared in the June 1982 issue of *Airman* Magazine.

Throughout its 65-year history Chanute has set the pace, not only as the oldest of five ATC technical training centers (the other four are at Keesler AFB, Mississippi; Lackland AFB, Texas; Lowry AFB, Colorado; and Sheppard AFB, Texas), but also as one of the Western World's largest and most progressive vocational training institutions. During six decades of operation the center has trained more than a million and a quarter students, many of whom went on to serve illustrious military careers. Graduates range from World War I aces to astronauts, and the center's roster or early commanders reads like a "Who's Who" in the history of aviation.

Chanute's current center commander, Maj. Gen. Norma E. Brown, is, herself, something of a pacesetter. During her 31-year, globe-trotting career, which began after she discovered that Air Force pay was twice what she was earning as a physical education instructor, she became the first woman blue-suiter to ever command a group, then a wing, and now a center. Today, she is also the highest-ranking woman in the Air Force.

Although the general, who's been called "Air Force's number one cheerleader," shrugs off her own accomplishments, she is quick to note that opportunities for women in today's Air Force are greater than ever. Currently, about 10 percent of the student population at Chanute is made up of women.

Her recipe for success? "Set professional, financial, and spiritual goals," she said, "but don't try to do something that you don't like to do. I tell my people that if you aren't happy during your first hitch, do a super job while you're in but get out after four (years) and find something that does make you happy. If they aren't happy in the Air Force, they won't do well and won't be self-fulfilled. It's that simple."

Maj. Gen. Brown's honesty and special ability to deal with people, coupled with a gracious homespun manner and charm, have made her popular on and off base. "I'm just a Florida sharecropper's daughter," she says humbly, "who, I guess, has a special feeling for every breathing soul." That explains, perhaps, her almost uncanny ability to remember forever, it seems, the first and last names of each person she meets. "A lot of people in this hurly-burly world are just in too much of a hurry and don't take the time to really listen to others," the general added. "I like people and pay attention to them—one at a time."

"I tell our graduates that their most important role as supervisors will be to care about their people and be team players," she said. "I'm not talking about babying and coddling. I'm talking about being sincere. If supervisors really care about their people, their folks will do a better job and have a greater feeling of pride in themselves and the unit. If they do that, each new assignment will be better than the last."

That, of course, is precisely how the general is approaching her current assignment, which, according to her, "is the best yet."

There is, certainly, a lot of pride at Chanute—pride in the base and in the job the center has been assigned to do. That the capability of the Air Force rests in the quality of its people is, it appears, the faculty's unspoken creed. For each faculty member knows that at the core of the Air Force's effectiveness is its highly skilled technicians, mechanics, and specialists.

"But," said Maj. Gen. Brown, "we have another mission here, which, I believe, is equally important—to provide continuation training in airmanship. That's important because the first thing the Air Force must have is officers and airmen who want to meet Air Force standards."

"Most of the students who come here do measure up and many have some definite goals in mind, such as gaining increased responsibility, a sense of personal accomplishment, or a skill they can use the rest of their lives. At Chanute, they can achieve all of those goals and more. In short, it can be the beginning of a challenging new way of life for them."

The Chaplain

Army Specialist Fifth Class Kathleen Ellison, reporting for the February 1983 issue of *Soldier, Sailor, Airman, Marine (SAM)*, related, "When the Army decided to promote Marilyn Henry they did it in a big way, jumping the 29-year-old from a private grease monkey to a lieutenant chaplain."

"I'm not even sure what happened myself," said Marilyn at Fort Leonard Wood, Missouri. "I was discharged from the Army as an enlisted soldier, then sworn in as an officer. When my orders first came in, people who didn't know me thought there must have been a mistake. 'Yes, I'm a woman chaplain and yes, my name is Marilyn Henry, not Henry Marilyn'."

Before signing on, Marilyn was a pastor for the Church of God in Anderson, Ind., for five years. There, she got her Master of Divinity degree from the School of Theology.

She wasn't sure what she wanted to do, so she took some vocational tests. The computer decided she was best suited to being a military officer.

"I had never considered the military," said Marilyn. "No one in my family had been in the military, none of my friends were in the military. I didn't even know anyone who had anything to do with the military." So Marilyn went into the military.

She chose the Army; and, although she could have had a direct commission, she wasn't sure the Army wanted to use her as a chaplain.

Marilyn's recruiter tried to talk her into being an airplane mechanic, but she figured, "How many people have a jet in their driveway? I want something I can use." She chose to be a light-wheeled-vehicle and power-generator mechanic.

The time soon came when Marilyn had to choose between being an enlisted mechanic or trying for the chaplaincy. "I think I would have liked staying in as an enlisted soldier," she said. "But I'm not getting any younger, and I definitely began to feel that there would be a place for me as a chaplain."

Private Henry put in her paperwork and the Army pushed it through.

Does Lieutenant Henry think her sex—there are fewer than a dozen female chaplains in the Army—will bring any special dimension to her Army ministry? "No," she said, "Male ministers have served women for years, so why should being a female minister serving men be any different? I'm sure the Army will have a tendency to send the problem female soldier to me, and I suppose there are some people who can talk to a woman more comfortably."

First Black Woman to Fly in Navy

Navy Ensign Brenda Robinson, profiled in the April 1981 issue of *All Hands* magazine, is not only one of the few women to have made inroads into what had previously been a male-dominated military field, but she also holds the distinction of being the first black female pilot in the Navy.

"All I ever wanted to do was fly," said the 24-year-old ensign of North Wales, Pennsylvania, who graduated from Dowling University. "I was one of only five women at Dowling pursuing a degree in aeronautics," she said. "By the time I graduated, I had flown solo and earned my private pilot's license." It wasn't until her senior year in college that she thought about flying military aircraft. "I was told I would have to spend two years in the Air Force before I could get into flight school. The Navy said if I was tough enough to get through its flight school, I could fly with them. The Navy issued a challenge that appealed to me."

She subsequently joined in November, 1978 and began Aviation Officer Candidate School in Pensacola shortly thereafter. "The first week was miserable," recalled Robinson. "I had asked myself what I was doing there." After completing the 16-week course, she received her commission as an officer and went on to primary flight training at Whiting Field, Florida and to advanced flight training at Corpus Christi, Texas. She was then awarded the wings of a naval aviator and was authorized to fly multi-engine, propeller-driven aircraft.

Assigned to fleet Logistics Support Squadron 40, Norfolk, Virginia, Brenda flies the C-1A Trader aircraft. The ensign doesn't enjoy being in the limelight, but would rather be left alone to "get the job done," as she puts it.

"I knew I was doing something unique and I realized I would be a pioneer," said the officer. "I also knew I would serve as an example. I hope other people will realize they, too, can do what I've done."

She Has Authority to Ground the Fleet

Air Force Master Sergeant Art Barnes, in the July 1982 issue of *Airman*, wrote about a woman lieutenant with exceptional responsibilities.

Under the stress of a short-field practice landing, an OV-10 *Bronco* forward air control aircraft suffered a cracked nose gear. 1st Lt. Judith E. Urey took a close look at the fork assembly, rose to her full 5 feet in height, and with a straight face told the deputy commander of maintenance at Sembach AB, West Germany, "Sir, we have to ground the fleet."

The colonel cringed, contemplating the impact of grounding the Air Force's 150-odd OV-10s for several months to refit them with stronger landing gear. And Urey recalls that the colonel wasn't smiling when she said, "Oh, I was only kidding. All we really have to do is restrict them.

What the young officer learned from the experience wasn't a joking matter.

"He took my word without question—me, a first lieutenant," said Urey in disbelief. "That was a surprise, but it also showed me how much stock the Air Force puts in the advice of its own engineers."

A year later the *Broncos* are still flying in Central Europe. They practice observing enemy positions and pinpointing targets for fighters and bombers—but they don't make short-field landings unless it's absolutely necessary.

At 27, 1st Lt. Urey is half of a two-person structural engineering team that makes such go or non-go decisions for flying units of the United States Air Forces in Europe. Until she joined him a year ago, Maj. Jim Bryant was a one-man engineering staff and had already served in Europe for two years following the opening of the Air Force Logistics Command's liaison office in 1979.

AFLC's European engineering mission has the same charter as Air Logistics Centers in the United States—to help maintenance crews at the Air Force's 20 flying bases in Europe solve aircraft repair problems not covered by technical orders. Maj. Bryant notes that he and 1st Lt. Urey have but one goal: to keep Air Force aircraft flying in Europe.

Some situations are outside the expertise of the two liaison officers or put an undue workload on them. When either happens, AFLC sends additional engineers to Europe. However, since the arrival of Urey last summer, the two-member team has been able to handle the entire workload although the pace is often hectic.

The two also provide a consultation service to maintenance teams working with aircraft accident investigation boards. For example, last winter 1st Lt. Urey traveled to Norvenich, an allied air base in northern Germany, to inspect an F-4 Aircraft. An engine explosion blew a 2-by-4-foot hole in the F-4's fuselage. She assessed the damage, estimated repairs, and designed an externally reinforced fuselage patch to enable the *Phantom* to return to Hahn AB.

She had no sooner returned home than she was on the go again, this time directed to a C-130 crash investigation at nearby Ramstein AB.

"We obviously keep busy," said the lieutenant, who holds a bachelor's degree in mechanical engineering, "but that's what's interesting about being a two-person AFLC engineering staff in Europe. I'm doing things a lot of my engineering classmates from Wichita (Kansas) State can only dream about. Some of them are still glorified draftsmen in civilian firms. Engineering challenges and responsibilities come a lot quicker in the Air Force."

She wanted a job that would challenge her math ability and make full use of her engineering degree. The lieutenant admits she initially entered the Air Force Reserve Officers' Training Corps program because she needed the $100-a-month ROTC stipend to help pay college expenses. But the program got her attention—and her interest—and she went on to become a distinguished ROTC graduate in 1978. Urey began her active-duty career as a structural engineer in the Ogden ALC at Hill AFB, Utah. Her specialty—the KC-135 landing gear.

"To a non-engineer, specializing in a landing gear may not sound like exciting work—but it was a real challenge."

She evaluated the *Stratotanker's* landing system to determine whether it could handle the stress of a newer, heavier model KC-135. "There was nothing wrong with the KC's old gear," she recalled, "but it couldn't stand the stress of the new aircraft—even though the newer-model KC-135 was only 800 pounds heavier."

1st Lt. Urey now uses her background in KC-135 landing, braking, and steering systems to help oversee some 750 aircraft stationed in Europe: 650 belonging to USAFE, 70 to the Military Airlift Command, and 30 to the Strategic Air Command.

The responsibility 1st Lt. Urey carries seems to perk her enthusiasm. "Engineering majors in college usually come into the Air Force either as development or systems engineers or as maintenance officers," she said. "My job at Ogden was fun—but this is even more fun, getting to know the nuts and bolts of different airplanes so I can make decisions for them to fly again. It's also given me a great feel for what it's like in the field, at the flying units. So in my job, I have the best of both worlds—engineering and maintenance. The responsibility and authority the Air Force and my major command have given me—a junior officer—is almost unbelievable."

Though the work is demanding, 1st Lt. Urey does find time to enjoy seeing Europe with her 9-year-old son, Robert.

"Europe has been a real experience for both of us. I'm enjoying it so much that I really haven't given much thought to where I'd like to be assigned when this tour is over. It's hard to think of a job that could top this one."

The Explosives Expert

What does a self-professed tomboy who likes working with mechanical things decide to be when she joins the Air Force?

Airman First Class Bonnie Richardson became an explosive ordnance disposal—EOD—specialist. In fact, there are only 54 women EOD types throughout the whole Defense Department. She's one of only 26 women in Air Force EOD.

EOD workers handle and dispose of old ammunition—safely. When bombs, rockets, or bullets outlive their shelf life, they're no longer considered safe and reliable. That's when Richardson and her fellow specialists use charges to blow up the old ammo at a nearby firing range.

Bonnie joined the Air Force right after high school, knowing she wanted to do something different.

Working in a mostly male job can be rough, but Richardson has overcome the obstacles. She says the rough language and constant teasing were the toughest things to deal with, but she learned to take them in stride.

As for the dangers of working with things that go "BOOM," Bonnie figures it isn't any more dangerous than driving a car. She says there isn't any more chance of getting hurt "as long as you do what you're supposed to do."

Airborne Private

Jerry Healy of Fort Bragg wrote about a private who might be small in stature, but is big on achievement, in the October 1983 issue of *Soldier, Sailor, Airman, Marine (SAM)*.

She's been called "shorty," "squirt," "short stuff," and other short names, but that doesn't really bother Private First Class Cynthia Beard of XVIII Airborne Corps' Casualty Office at Fort Bragg, N.C.

"Actually, it kind of makes me feel good," she says. "I may be little, but people notice me."

The 5′2″ Airborne soldier seems to have made it a point to be noticed during her 1½ years in the Army.

A sign of her most recent accomplishment is neatly stitched atop her right fatigue pocket. The large green wings signify completion of Canadian Jump School, and are worn by only one other female outside Canada.

Beard's brief military career has been impressive, especially her achievement as a parachutist.

Following her "Soldier of the Cycle" award, out of about 200 soldiers in basic training, the 106-pound Beard progressed to Advanced Individual Training, where she was again awarded top honors.

In American jump school, out of approximately 145 soldiers, Beard and an Air Force colonel were certified distinguished honor graduates. Approximately 25 soldiers failed to even complete the training.

"When I go through a course, I don't say, 'well, I want to

come out number one,' " she said. "I just want to do as well as I can do."

Words such as "go-getter," "positive attitude," and "hard charger" often surface when co-workers speak of Beard. She concedes it's probably her general attitude that leads her to excel.

Yet, she adds that her persistence has also helped her attain some of her goals. "You're not going to get anything by standing back. There's a time to be quiet and a time to be loud."

Private First Class Beard plans to stay in the Army. She's begun a night class and intends to take more courses. "I'd like to be an officer," she says. "Yeah, I think that would be neat."

The Grand Old Lady of Computers

Grace Hopper isn't what you might expect. That was Seaman Steve Johnson's reaction as he wrote about her in the September 1982 issue of *All Hands* magazine.

Think of a computer specialist and a person hunched over an electronic calculator spouting technical jargon immediately comes to mind. Think of Captain Grace Hopper and you'll recall some anecdotes she reels off like a seasoned entertainer delivering one liners.

At age 77, Hopper is anything but conventional.

On the final day of a recent Navywide microcomputer workshop in Virginia Beach, Virginia, Hopper captivated her audience of nearly 300 computer professionals. They sat at rapt attention as she proclaimed the future possibilities of the computer age, along with some of the problems.

Hopper began her talk by poking fun at herself, recounting the recent embarrassment of being mistaken for an airport security guard. Since then, she makes sure she keeps her Navy hat on whenever she travels, but even that has had its drawbacks.

"I was moving through a baggage check point once when a man there asked if I was in the Navy," she recalls. "I promptly answered 'Yes!' He looked me up and down for a long time without saying a word, then replied, 'You must be the oldest one they've got!' "

Actually, she *is* the oldest Navy person on active duty now that Admiral Hyman Rickover has left active duty. Hopper is to the automated data processing community a walking, talking, living legend. In May, 1983, *Newsweek* magazine called her "The Grand Old Lady of Computers."

Born on December 9, 1906, in New York, Grace Hopper came into a world much different from today's. The automobile and the aeroplane were mechanical gadgets operated by daredevils; the Great White Fleet would sail from Hampton Roads in 1907; and she would turn 8 years old before Alexander Graham Bell could make the first transcontinental telephone call from New York to San Francisco.

She attended Vassar College and was graduated Phi Beta Kappa in 1928. The fellowship she earned led her to Yale University, where she received a master's degree in 1930 and a Ph.D. in 1934, along with election to Sigma Xi and two Sterling Scholarships.

In 1931, Grace Hopper returned to Vassar as an assistant in the mathematics department, becoming, successively, instructor, assistant professor and associate professor. She then received a faculty fellowship and chose to study at New York University (1941-42).

With the world at war, Hopper entered the Naval Reserve in December 1943. She attended the Midshipman's School at Northhampton, Massachusetts. Upon graduation, she was commissioned a lieutenant junior grade with orders to the Bureau of Ordnance's computation project at Harvard. It was there that she would become only the third person ever to program the first large-scale digital computer, Mark I.

In a few years, the Mark I was a museum piece; in its place stood UNIVAC I. "A thousand times faster," proclaimed Hopper. "Unless you saw those early computers, you can't really appreciate what today's microcomputer can do."

At that time, a myriad of computer languages were cropping up to be run on these new offspring of technology. The problem was that those diverse languages were incompatible. The computer age was on the verge of collapse.

Hopper knew what was needed: a compiler, a sort of translator that would alter a source program into an object program capable of being run on a particular computer. The naysayers groused, "It can't be done." Hopper said, "It can so."

The world's first compiler, the A-0 system, was developed by Hopper and her staff at Remington in 1952.

Her appointment as staff scientist, systems programming, at Sperry Rand in 1964 just preceded the third, and current, generation of computer hardware introduced in 1966—computers built around silicon chips, but still dependent on the compilers Hopper and her staff pioneered.

Throughout all of this, Grace Hopper maintained her close connection with the Naval Reserve and was subsequently promoted to commander. At the end of 1966, she was retired in that rank, proclaiming it "The saddest day of my life." But in less than a year, she was recalled to active duty. By 1973, she was promoted to the rank of captain on the retired list of the Naval Reserve. Currently, she is serving on active duty with the Naval Data Automation Command.

Nearly 40 years after this woman converted the Navy to the computer age, Captain Grace Hopper stood before her audience, extolling the virtues of the bigger and better computers to come, and the impact they will have on our world.

She predicted "tremendous changes on the horizon" in the way we process information.

To give credence to her call for new, more sophisticated computers, Hopper cited several seemingly unrelated instances where large systems of computers will be needed to head off worldwide crises.

"The population of the world is increasing, as is the need to increase the world's food supply," she said.

Long-range weather forecasts will help facilitate plans for planting crops, she explained. Water allocation will also prove to be a major computer effort.

"Bigger systems of computers are needed now," she said.

Captain Hopper is as vocal about her ideas of management as she is about computers. On that subject, Hopper listed her "three-point plan" for improving office efficiency:

"One—supervisors should listen to their juniors. Two—juniors should never quit after the first 'no.' And three—juniors should work to educate their superiors."

"We have to be a little slippery in educating our bosses," she remarked.

What's her tried and true secret?

No secret, she said. "Let the boss think it's all his idea."

She concluded, "I've spent many years in the busiest, best field, receiving every kind of award available. But the highest award I have received is serving proudly in the U.S. Navy."

The Military Commitment

> **Oath of Enlistment**
>
> I, Jane Doe, do solemnly swear (or affirm) that I will support and defend the Constitution of the United States against all enemies, foreign and domestic; that I will bear true faith and allegiance to the same; that I will obey the orders of the officers appointed over me, according to regulations and the Uniform Code of Military Justice. SO HELP ME GOD.

The Oath of Enlistment (for officers, the Oath of Office) you will take upon entering the Armed Forces symbolizes a commitment. This commitment involves much more than just your pledge that you will give two or more years in service to your country. It means that you commit yourself to support and defend the Constitution of the United States against all enemies. You are stating under oath your commitment to have faith in and pay allegiance to the Constitution. Finally, you are promising to obey the orders of your military superiors.

Read the words in the Oath of Enlistment carefully. You'll see that this is a solemn and serious commitment not to be taken lightly. Many Americans in three world wars and some 36 major conflicts have given their lives in keeping faith with this oath. Millions of others have served in uniform with honor and distinction. In taking the Oath of Enlistment, you join these many men and women who have selflessly and devotedly sacrificed for their country.

The decision of whether or not to join military service is, in the end, up to you. The armed forces offer women exceptional opportunities. Job training, adequate and secure salary, and a multitude of benefits such as cost-free education, travel, and friendships—all of these and more can be yours. But the military also offers you a rare opportunity to serve your country by becoming a member of the most important group in our society: the military profession. The Oath you take will be your initiation into this profession.

Bon voyage! The next chapter is yours to write.

Index

N

O

P

R

S

T

U

V

W

Y

Acknowledgements

The authors would like to express their appreciation to the following individuals and organizations for their assistance in providing information for this book: Anna C. Urband, Media Services Branch, U.S. Navy Office of Information; Jan K. Herman, Historian, Naval Medical Command; Major F. C. Bash, Division of Public Affairs, U.S. Marine Corps; MSgt. William R. McKenzie, Office of Public Affairs, Bergstrom Air Force Base, Texas; Dorothy Frooks, Women World War Veterans; the Media, Books, and Magazines Division of both the U.S. Army and U.S. Air Force offices of public affairs; and the military recruiting services of the five military branches.

We are especially grateful to Bettie Sprigg, Office of the Assistant Secretary of Defense for Public Affairs. Ms. Sprigg not only assisted in our search for information within the Department of Defense, but also arranged for the various branches of service to provide the photographs that are displayed throughout the book.

The authors used a variety of service publications in researching, including *Profile, Airman, Soldier* and *All Hands* magazines. *Soldier, Sailor, Airman, Marine (Sam)* magazine continues to publish a vigorous "Letters to the Editor" column, from which we extracted numerous quotes.

A special word of thanks goes to Jeanne Holm, Major General, USAF (Retired). General Holm's excellent book, *Women in the Military* (Presidio Press, 1982), provided the authors with insight into the history of women's progress toward equal opportunity in the armed forces and jogged our thinking processes as we wrote about current issues and controversies regarding women in the military.

Finally, our gratitude to Wanda Marrs who formatted and reviewed our manuscript and made many valuable suggestions.